D1562369

JUAREZ

MAN OF LAW

by Elizabeth Borton de Treviño

Elizabeth Borton de Treviño

JUAREZ

MAN OF LAW

FARRAR, STRAUS AND GIROUX • NEW YORK

Library of Congress Cataloging in Publication Data
Treviño, Elizabeth Borton
Juárez, man of law.
Bibliography: p.
1. Juárez, Benito Pablo, Pres. Mexico, 1806–1872—Juvenile
literature. [1. Juárez, Benito Pablo, Pres. Mexico, 1806–1872.
2. Mexico—Presidents] I. Title.
F1233.J95463   972'.07'0924 [B]   74–12012
ISBN 0–374–33950–3

To my son
LIC. ENRIQUE TREVIÑO BORTON,
whose help has been invaluable
in the preparation of this book

The life of Juárez has been told here with careful adherence to known facts. In order to make the personality of the Benemérito more vivid, the author has added to each chapter a visualized scene, which is an expression of the author's imagination, a projection of some important moment in the past which affected Juárez in one way or another.

The serious biography is not disturbed in any way by the author's extraneous interpolations; yet some emotional content in the extra scenes may, she hopes, awaken in readers something of her own feeling about the great Mexican president.

CONTENTS

CONTENTS

FOREWORD

There are many kinds of heroes. Some are spectacular personalities who envision and carry out daring deeds for the good of their country and their neighbors. Others are wily fighters who devise campaigns to defeat the enemy. Still others have great powers of leadership, the ability to arouse loyalty and to excite their followers to brilliant action.

Usually a national hero—a man who comes to be all that the people think of as an inspiring example—is a man of aggressive nationalism or of military genius, like Washington, Bolivar, or Garibaldi. Very often, too, the hero is a martyr, dying for his cause, like Lincoln or Martin Luther King.

There are exceptions. An outstanding one is that of Benito Juárez, who was president of Mexico during

years of great stress and trouble but who was not a uniformed soldier. Simple, dignified, and modest, he did
not arouse followers to great glories through oratory.
He was not a martyr; he survived the crises in his life
and died naturally of a heart ailment. His hero and
friend was Lincoln.

Juárez became a great national hero, revered not only
by Mexicans, who have made his birthday a national
holiday, but also by all the nationalities of Latin America, who call him *Benemérito de las Americas* (worthy
hero of the Americas). He is regarded as a hero because he was stubbornly devoted to the idea that strict
observance of the law is what makes men worthy, that
law is the greatest achievement of men in their efforts
to live together peacefully on this earth, and that justice
must be the same for everyone.

Juárez was a lawmaker. But most of all, he was a Man
of the Law.

Yet this remarkable person began life as a poor
shepherd in the hills of southern Mexico. He was pure
Zapotec Indian, a race that had no privileges and no
power whatever in the Mexico of that day (Juárez was
born in 1806), and until he was almost thirteen, he did
not even speak Spanish.

But just as the seed mysteriously holds within itself
the secret knowledge of the plant or the tree it will be-

come, so that little Indian shepherd held within his character and his intelligence the man who was to become
president of Mexico, a national hero, and the "Benemérito de las Americas."

JUAREZ

MAN OF LAW

ONE

Childhood Years

BENITO JUÁREZ was a Zapotec Indian boy who lived
with his grandfather in the village of Guelatao, in the
mountains of Oaxaca, Mexico. While the grandfather
tilled a small plot of land, the boy tended their sheep.

When the hills were green with good pasture and his
sheep cropped the sweet grass, Benito might sit on a
rock, his crook beside him, and dream of the past glories
of the Zapotec nation, and remember all the tales his
grandfather had told him. The Zapotecans had been
great rulers, poets, philosophers, and astronomers before the conquering Spanish had arrived to reduce them
to poverty and servitude.

Benito learned patience, as shepherds are patient, for
time goes slowly. The sun rises, moves overhead, casts
short shadows and then long dark ones before it is time
to lead the gentle sheep home.

Shepherds must be loyal and vigilant, for sheep are both timid and easily panicked, and they are subject to various dangers. A rattlesnake may be trod upon and strike back. A hungry mountain lion may find a tree or overhanging rock on which to crouch and await some straggler. The shepherd must have keen eyes and be brave and resourceful, to protect his animals.

The shepherd must have knowledge of the country where he roams, must know where he can take his sheep to shelter in the event of a sudden storm, where he can always find water for them, paths which may take them home in the shadowy cool of the evening, and warm dells where they can be protected from the cold wind.

All these things the boy Benito Juárez learned in his childhood, and he never forgot them. When the day came that he had to call upon these qualities, in order to lead his countrymen out of danger and toward his ideal of a free country, with justice for all, they were part of his character.

What did he look like, this shepherd child? He was short, with a strong, wiry body, dark skin, straight black hair that stuck up through his ragged straw hat, and very black eyes that looked both bright and thoughtful. He wore pants and a blouse made of heavy white cotton (which was not washed too often, for it was his only clothing), and a poncho or cape, which was woven of rough wool that kept the rain out. He was usually bare-

foot, and his small square feet were toughened and cal-
loused from walking over gravel and rocks.

A boy in the mountain village of Guelatao had a hard
life by our standard today. He was very poor, his diet
was monotonous—usually boiled beans and corn tortillas
—he was often hungry, he had to work, and he had little
time to play. Of course, he did play, like all children, in
snatched hours. Undoubtedly he sat by the side of a
small, beautiful lake near the village and dreamed of a
better life.

The greatest lack was education. In the early part of
the nineteenth century, when he was born, Mexico was
still a colony of Spain's. There were few schools of any
kind, and almost none for Indian children, who, in any
case, had to learn Spanish before they could enter. Kind
missionaries taught where they could, but they could
not be everywhere. Young Benito felt most bitterly the
need for school, for an education, because he was intelligent and he knew that he could never change or
better his life until he had an education, which would
give him the tools he needed for progress—a knowledge
of Spanish and a profession.

In a book of notes which he himself set down for his
children, in later years, he wrote that his uncle, with
whom he lived, taught him the rudiments of reading.
And he learned some Spanish words, many from the
men who came through the village with burroloads of

cloth and cutlery to sell, and who left with loads of wool from the Guelatao sheep.

Benito had security, in the sense that he was deeply loved by his family. Tragedy overtook it when he was tiny; this was often the case among the poor Indian families of the mountains. His mother died giving birth to a baby girl, and his father died not long after. The village was small; there were only twenty families in Guelatao, among them relatives to take in the small orphan boy. Benito, not yet three, was welcomed into the humble home of his grandfather. But he also died, and the child, who was so familiar with death, who saw so many of his dear ones lowered into the earth, wrapped in a straw petate, went to live with an uncle, Bernardino Juárez.

The child came to love this uncle very dearly. He told Benito much historical lore about the Zapotec nation, and until the day of his death, Benito Juárez never forgot that he came of a great people, who were different from the Spaniards and who had been conquered, but who were admirable. He never in his life felt inferior, no matter what he had to do. It has been said that one cannot be made to feel inferior unless one consents. He never consented.

The only way to get an education in the Spanish-speaking schools of Oaxaca City, Benito knew, was by going to the "big city" and working in the home of someone who would allow him time off to attend classes. This was the system by which some of the children of Guelatao and other mountain villages managed to get an education. Benito's own sister, Josefa, was working as a cook in the family of an Italian named Maza.

Between the ages of ten and twelve, Benito had a long, painful struggle between his ambitious dreams and his longing to learn, and his love for his family and his friends. His uncle, however, pointed out to him that the only way for an Indian to achieve an education and a career was to go to a Church school and study to be a priest.

Many years later, Juárez wrote to his children that it was a "cruel struggle" for him to decide to leave his uncle, who had been so good to him, and his friends. But one day, with characteristic courage, he walked out of his home and took the road to Oaxaca. He wrote that he arrived in Oaxaca "on the same day, at night." As the distance is about seventy miles, perhaps some cart or horseman gave the boy a lift. Or perhaps he left home at night and walked steadily. In any case, he knew where to go. His sister Josefa awaited him, and there, in the large, comfortable home of the Maza family, he found refuge.

Not long after he found a friend and protector named Antonio Salanueva. This gentleman was a bookbinder, and a devoted, practicing Catholic. He wore the habit of the Third Order of Franciscans (an order of lay people who do not live in a monastery but who cooperate with the priests and nuns) and did much charitable work. Don Antonio believed firmly that all children should be educated. He took Benito in, and in exchange for some simple work—sweeping out the patio and running errands—he gave him a home and sent him to school.

Don Antonio Salanueva, like Benito's uncle, hoped that the bright and serious boy would want to study for holy orders. Benito, too, had this idea at first, out of affection for his protector.

Benito continued to visit Don Antonio Maza, in whose home he was always cordially received, and as the boy grew, he looked upon him as a friend.

As it might have been . . .

A simple Mexican Indian woman stands before a table slicing onions. The room is large and should be spacious, but it is cluttered with the implements of cooking. All along one side, at waist level, is a charcoal stove, lined with brilliantly colored tiles; openings below admit the charcoal, and the fuel is kept at red heat by air fanned into the hole with woven straw fans. Two little girls are doing this, while the cook continues to slice her onions. On the floor is a big stone metate, on which the cook will grind corn, kneeling to do so, as her people have done for centuries. Standing about on tables and shelves are stone mortars and pestles, in which various spices, chilis, and vegetables are reduced to a puree. The walls are hung with clay cooking pots of many sizes and designs, and strung across the ceiling are lines of drying chili peppers, strings of garlic, and bunches of herbs. The whole room smells of the hot corn tortillas cooking on the stove, of the spicy chilis and savory meat stewing in a clay pot.

The cook is a short woman, very thin and dark. She wears a flowered cotton skirt, two aprons, one on top of the other, and a short-sleeved blouse. She is not a pretty woman; she has a stern, intelligent face and smiles very infrequently. Her hair, straight and black, is in two braids down her back, tied together at the ends with a piece of colored wool.

It is the evening supper hour, and the dark has come down outside. Through the open door and windows, the cook can barely discern the well in the back patio; she can just hear the stamping of the horses in their stalls as the animals are given their oats and hay.

Suddenly in the doorway appears a small figure. It is a little boy, an Indian child, wearing worn and dusty white cotton clothes, a tattered straw hat, and a woven poncho. He says nothing, just stands and waits. The child's face is tired and drawn but resolute; there are no tears in his steady, shining dark eyes.

"Benito!" says the cook, and then the child smiles, hopefully, and steps toward his sister.

"Josefa," he says.

She hugs him, presses him close for a moment.

"I have come," he says simply.

TWO

First Disillusions and Difficulties

T HE MAN who, in years to come, was to be a great re-
former of laws that oppressed some of the people and
permitted injustice came very early to have an idea of
what was fair and just.

The little Indian boy whose Spanish, as he admitted
later, was vulgar and ungrammatical when he was
twelve went to school under the protection of Sr. Salanueva. He was full of hope and energy and was longing to learn. But he found out, to his dismay, that
Spanish as a language was not taught in the elementary
school. All that was taught was a catechism written by
Padre Ripalda, which the pupils were expected to copy
and learn by heart. Benito had enough judgment to
know that this was not going to be the education he
wanted, and he begged to be transferred. He was reg-
istered in another school and asked what grade he

thought he should enter. He answered, "Fourth." He was then told to write out a page of composition, in Spanish. Of course, he did this very poorly, and his teacher, instead of correcting him, became annoyed, told him that his composition was unacceptable, and ordered him punished. What this punishment was, Benito did not say in his letters to his children, written many decades later, but one can see that the memory of this injustice offended him and hurt him deeply, for he never forgot it.

The world was also teaching the child from the mountain village many other things, and recurring injustices were part of them. He had entered a school called the Royal School, where he observed that there was one teacher who worked in a separate classroom, with the well-dressed children of well-to-do Spanish families. In another room, a less-prepared person known as a "helper" taught the poor children who were sent there, mostly Indian servant children.

In disgust and disillusion, Benito left school and made up his mind to study alone and to practice writing and reading until he could express himself correctly in Spanish. With difficulty, but with persistence, he did.

Thus, from his earliest years, Benito Juárez became aware of injustices and of the separation of people into privileged classes and classes that were considered to have no rights at all. At the same time, his judgment became clear, and he was not content merely to rage against what he knew was not fair. He looked for a solution, found one, and settled down to it, though it was a difficult one. He was not one to give up.

While he worked for his board and room and studied by himself, and while he ran errands in the city for his protector or patron, Benito began to realize that there was still another possibility for him. He could receive a good education if he decided to enter the seminary and study for holy orders, as his uncle had always advised.

Spanish laws, so unequal in many other ways, were at least reasonable insofar as they dealt with young men preparing for the priesthood. Indian priests were encouraged. The fact that a young man knew and spoke one of the Indian tongues was considered to be a "patrimony," and upon completing his studies, he could be ordained a priest without having to give the Church a fixed sum of money to live on until he was appointed to a parish.

When Benito began to consider studying for the priesthood, his benefactor, being a religious man, was delighted that his protégé might go into the Church. He pointed out to Benito that his knowledge of the Zapotecan language would be greatly to his advantage, as he could work among his own people.

Benito, though he felt little inclination for the re-

ligious life, saw that this was his best opportunity;
therefore he began studying in the seminary. Very
happy at his studies, he learned Latin and looked forward to studying philosophy and literature. His patron,
Sr. Salanueva, soon began pressing him to take the short
course in moral theology and thus be ordained earlier,
but Benito convinced him that it would be better to receive a complete education before deciding for holy
orders. Then, if he did wish to become a priest, he would
have sufficient preparation to be really useful, whereas
many of the priests with short grounding in Latin and
theology were widely known to be pitifully ignorant.

Thus, four years later, Benito graduated from a course
in arts and letters with high honors. He was twenty-one
years old. And in the Maza household a little girl had
been born, named Margarita. In years to come, Benito
watched the little girl grow up, and he loved her, first
as a child and a little girl, and later as a young woman.

Meanwhile, great changes were taking place in Mexico, and the studious, dedicated young man, with his
strong sense of justice, was aware of them.

As it might have been . . .

It is a dark rainy night in Oaxaca, past ten o'clock. Church bells sound, marking the hour, from a church nearby; they are heard in the room where a dark young boy sits studying at a table. The room is furnished very simply with a plain narrow bed, spread with dark woolen sarapes, a table, and a chair. On the table are many books, writing paper, and pens. A single candle burns, to give light on the book the boy is holding in his hands. Above the bed hangs a large crucifix, for this is a Catholic home. The boy wears a plain white shirt and white cotton trousers, but he has a warm dark-gray poncho over his shoulders. He is barefoot. Around his neck, on a silver chain, hangs a holy medal, the gift of his protector, who has hopes that the boy may eventually take holy orders and go as a priest to his people.

Benito studies, and then, setting aside his book, he carefully and slowly practices writing.

There is a knock at the door, and a voice says, "Benito?"

The boy springs up, walks across the cold floor, feeling nothing, for he is not used to shoes.

"Benito, my boy. Time to go to bed."

"Sí, Don Antonio. At once."

Obediently, Benito blows out his candle, but before

getting into bed, he goes to the window. The rain is rattling on the tiled roof with a sound like pebbles falling, and there is a continual chuckling gurgling from the water spouts, which are pouring rainwater into barrels set below to catch the soft "water from the sky."

Another day, the boy thinks. Every day I must make some progress. Every day.

At last he turns aside, kneels swiftly to say night prayers, and then cuddles under the warm sarape. In the darkness, with the sound of the rain continuing, he falls asleep.

THREE

A Man of Law

In 1810, when Benito was only four years old, the first struggles to free Mexico from the domination of Spain took place. Two idealistic priests, Miguel Hidalgo and José María Morelos, had led the difficult and unequal struggle against the armies of the King of Spain. They wanted Mexico to become a nation, with the same opportunities and advantages for all citizens—but they were defeated, humiliated, and put to death. Their followers became discouraged and disbanded.

But the idea of freedom from Spain did not die out. In 1820, the rebellion flared up again, under the leadership of Agustín Iturbide, a flamboyant, aristocratic figure who soon (in 1822) proclaimed himself emperor of the new free Mexico.

Benito Juárez was only sixteen when this happened, but he was in school and had been learning. No doubt

17.

he was at least superficially aware of the fact that the Spaniards, who had conquered Mexico, were at last to lose their power over the country and over his people.

However, it was soon apparent that Mexico, free from Spain, was only another little Spain, under the power of the Emperor Iturbide. Benito, remembering the traditions of the glorious Zapotec nation, before defeat by the Spanish, could not see that there was much hope that his people could rise again to a position of trust and dignity. No doubt he thought much about the changes going on around him, but while he had no interest at all in maintaining the privileges of the rich and educated over the poor and ignorant, he was wise enough to keep his mind on his studies, to say little, and to listen and remember. He had the hope that a more just system of law and education in Mexico would come out of the Independence and the various congresses that issued proclamations and the treaties that attempted to set up systems and laws.

One thing happened in Oaxaca that was to his advantage. Freedom from Spain and from Church control of education led, in 1827, to the establishment in the city of a liberal lay college (Civil College). Benito was then twenty-one years old, still longing for learning, still willing to make all kinds of sacrifices to achieve a real education. He wished to enter the Civil College and study law, but he had the hard task of convincing the kind man who had stood by him and helped him all along the way to education. Sr. Salanueva was sad when Benito told him that he felt he had no vocation for the priesthood and wanted to study law, but being naturally generous, Don Antonio gave his consent.

Now the young Indian from the hills learned that privileges and persecution did not automatically cease with a change of government. The conservatives in Mexico—people who had property and privileges they wished to conserve—did not like the idea of a liberal, lay college, which might undermine their special advantages by teaching young lawyers how to combat them. And so they began a program of persecution of the Civil College. Many students became discouraged or frightened and left. But Benito Juárez remained in the college, enduring rocks thrown at him, campaigns of slander against him, and shouted and printed insults.

It must be remembered that he had nothing to lose. He was of a race that had been humiliated and reduced to abject poverty and the status of servants. He had everything to gain by persisting in his wish to achieve a good education and a profession. Thus, he remained in the college, with typical perseverance and patience, qualities that were to distinguish him all his life.

In the Colegio Civil, besides studying law, he learned modern languages, political economy, jurisprudence, comparative systems of law, and natural, civil, and constitutional law. His mind, naturally calm and cool, developed into a positive, active, and rational instrument; it was to be a help and a defense for him all of his life.

In 1831, when he was twenty-five, he entered a Oaxaca law office and began to practice. Naturally, his clients were mostly poor, and mostly Indians like himself. But he was able to begin earning a living, and the whole pattern of his life and of his basic character took form. He became a man of law, a man who respected and loved the idea of a code of law—a constitution and laws which were accepted by the people, by which they could live with each other in peace and honor—and a system of courts to administer them, to assure equal justice for all.

The Indian boy from the hills, to whom organized religion had no direct appeal (though he remained respectful of the *spiritual* office of the Church), put all his hope and all his devotion into the idea of law . . . man-made law . . . to which all citizens must conform, but which, at the same time, protected and defended all.

As the life and the history of Benito Juárez developed, this thread ran through it, unbroken: a love of law itself, and a loving respect for law.

He became in every way a Man of Law.

As it might have been . . .

The scene is a law office in the old city of Oaxaca. There is a large reception room, with a tall counter barring the public from the rooms beyond. Straight wooden chairs around the walls are for clients awaiting appointments. The floor is tiled; the roof is high; the windows onto an inner courtyard, through which a pale light enters, are narrow. It is broad daylight outside, but in this office there is a musty darkness; the place smells of old books, old leather bindings; every time a door to the inner offices is opened, the fragrance of a cigar steals out to mix with the dusty fragrance of the books.

A young man has appeared in the doorway. He is short, dark, clean-shaven. Dressed in a sober suit of black wool, he wears a spotless white shirt with stiff collar, a dark tie, and black shoes. He gleams with polish; his hair, black and straight, has been brushed flat; the whites of his black eyes shine like china. His hands, small, compact brown hands, are very clean, and his shoes have been polished until they reflect light.

An old Indian, in a clean and starched white cotton suit of homemade shirt and trousers that tie on around the waist, barefoot, with his straw hat in his work-worn hands, gets up at the sight of the young man in black and takes his hand as if to kiss it.

The young lawyer gently takes his hand away and bows respectfully to the Indian.

"Come into my office, Don Nacho," he says to the old Indian, in a pleasant baritone voice, "and we will discuss your problem."

They pass into one of the inner rooms, the young lawyer opening the door for his client and quietly waiting, with respect, for him to pass through first.

The door closes softly behind them, but not before the lawyer, Benito Juárez, has said, "How can I serve you, Don Nacho? I am here to help you."

FOUR

Beginning Politics and Marriage

I N THE next ten years of his life, Benito Juárez entered politics and began to learn how the law operates. At first, he was an alderman of the municipality, where he came into contact with some of the political struggles for power that were going on in his native country.

While free from Spain, Mexico had as yet no settled government, for Iturbide, who had declared himself emperor, had fallen from grace and had been exiled by the congress. When he tried to return to Mexico, he had been captured, judged, and executed. A new power arose in the military leader General Antonio López de Santa Anna, a colorful and domineering personality, who at first had been content to defend the struggling new constitutional republic, but who soon revealed himself as a man who wanted power for himself.

Juárez, from his position as a small officeholder in the

city of Oaxaca, saw how Santa Anna came to Oaxaca to help in forcing the election of Vicente Guerrero as president of Mexico; he also saw how Guerrero was deposed, pursued to Oaxaca again, and killed there. Juárez began to get the idea that men fought each other to manipulate votes as much as they had ever done to get power by force of arms. And sometimes they used arms to get the *apparent* ratification of ballots.

Santa Anna finally managed to get himself elected president of Mexico in 1833. However, he was intelligent enough to know that he was gifted only in military affairs. Therefore, it was his vice-president, Dr. Valentín Gómez Farias, who formulated and put through many liberal reforms. The Church was no longer to be allowed to use civil police to pursue persons who had not paid their tithes; the state was to control the sale of Church property; no more burials were to be allowed inside churches; the state was to regulate education.

All this seems natural to us now, and it is strange to think that things were different for so long in Mexico when it was under Spain and during the first struggles of the country to become a free republic.

Juárez, unburdened as he was by any previous special privileges, was in favor of all these liberal reforms, and under a liberal banner he was elected to the state congress in Oaxaca. One of the first motions he made was to confiscate the land of the conqueror Cortes on behalf of the state. The conqueror had been named "Marquis of the Valley of Oaxaca," and enormous tracts of land granted to him under the Spanish crown were still respected, until Juárez took legal steps to return the land to the people.

In his law practice, Juárez learned that special privilege, a situation which he felt deeply was against all principles of law, still operated within the system of the courts. He was representing some villagers against a priest who had been extorting money from them, but while the case was pending, the president was changed, and in the confusion, the angry priest jailed all the defendants and also their lawyer, Juárez. Juárez spent nine days in jail until the Supreme Court, to which he appealed, released him and his clients. No more was heard of the matter.

Juárez had to learn painfully of the existence of such injustice. As he wrote, later, when liberal government followed conservative government, "Only persons were changed, the laws were not changed, and certain classes retained their immunity and their privileges."

This, and other experiences, made him dedicate himself, forever after, even more devotedly to the law. Not merely was he dedicated—as a teacher, lawyer, and magistrate—to the observance of existing laws, but his mind was made up to try to see that good and fair laws, which were to be applied without privilege or immunity for anyone, became part of the patrimony of his country.

In 1843, Juárez married the little girl he had watched grow up, Margarita Maza, the daughter of the employers of his sister, his own friends and patrons. What did he look like, this young Zapotec lawyer, self-made, who came courting the daughter of the rich Italian merchant? She said, in writing to a friend about her approaching marriage: "He is very homely, but he is very good."

She loved him, and she saw beyond outward appearances. In fact, he was short, dark, squarely built, strong, with straight black hair cut short and parted on the side, a wide mouth, and black eyes. He was never to change very much, only to grow a bit stouter in his final years. He remained clean-shaven all his life. His best feature was his shining dark eyes, which saw everything, but which were patient, kept many secrets. His voice was reported as a firm, pleasant baritone, which carried well when he made speeches.

A photograph taken of the bride, who was seventeen, and the bridegroom, thirty-seven, shows a lovely young woman, with a pale, oval face; dark, curling hair; and a bemused look of love in her dark eyes. Juárez, too, looks young and romantic in the photograph, with an expression on his face which seems to express his gratitude and his pride at having the luck to win a girl like Margarita.

The marriage was a very happy one. Margarita loved her husband devotedly and helped him in every way she could, all her life. As for him, he adored his wife, and when she died, he did not long survive her.

As it might have been . . .

The sala of the Maza house in Oaxaca City is large and spacious, with four big windows facing directly on the square. The windows are barred, but there is no impression of a prison, for each window has a deep seat, with a padded velvet cushion, and thick velvet drapes give an effect of comfort and luxury. In the exact center of the room, standing on the fine French carpet, is a delicate inlaid table, and leaning against this table are four beautifully embroidered silk cushions. Large carved armchairs with dark-red silk cushions stand about, and in a corner of the spacious room is a square piano, with mother-of-pearl keys. A chandelier with candle sconces and many sparkling prisms hangs above the table. Against the walls, covered with a wallpaper representing French scenes, are several portraits of dignified gentlemen in dark suits and of sweet-faced women in high-necked dresses. The portraits look out upon the only occupant of the room. He is a rather short, dark, quiet gentleman, dressed in sober black. He holds his silk hat in his hand; his black hair shines in the light from the chandelier. Though his face is calm and impassive, one can see that he is nervous, for he walks up and down in an agitated manner, rounding the little table time and again.

Suddenly there is a rustle of silk skirts, a little choked giggle, and a breath of rose perfume. A young girl stands in the doorway, gazing at the man with a look of mischief and delight. She is short and very slender, with white skin, dark, softly curling hair, an oval face, a sweet, small mouth, now punctuated at each corner by a deep dimple. She is wearing a dress of silk in changeable shades of rose and gold. It is made tight through the bodice, clinging close to a willowy young waist, and above the hem (which almost conceals the little feet in black satin slippers) are loops and festoons of black velvet ribbon. Around her neck she wears a gold chain, from which hangs a little garnet cross.

"Nito!" She runs to him, arms outstretched, and he takes her hands closely into his own. His expression seems not to change, but his dark shining eyes never leave her large soft brown ones.

He clears his throat and speaks carefully, "Margarita, your father has given me permission . . ."

"I know!" She is laughing delightedly into his face.

"To . . . to . . ."

"To kiss me, Nito?"

"To ask you to be my wife!"

"When I say yes . . and I shall say it in a minute . . . then you must kiss me, Nito! Oh, I am so happy! Do you love me? I know you do! Kiss me now! Yes, yes, Nito! I have loved you for so long!"

FIVE

Governor of Oaxaca

Ɪɴ 1841, Juárez was appointed a judge, but when he was ordered by President Santa Anna to prosecute persons who did not pay their Church tithes, he resigned. Shortly after this, he was returned to the bench and promoted to the State Supreme Court. In 1845, he was elected to the local legislature, and soon after he was elected to the national congress, which was called by Santa Anna to meet in Mexico City.

His preparation had been slow and careful. First, an education, by whatever means he could find, in difficult times. Then a degree in law, and practice, where he learned that even within the law, the poor were often the victims of the powerful. Then a judgeship, which gave him training in the administration of the law. And then, finally, to the legislature and the national congress, where he could take part in the *making of law*.

This was his passion, and indeed, he dedicated the rest of his life to the making of law, and to insistence that laws be respected and obeyed.

Laws, he demonstrated throughout his life, are man's attempt to secure justice and fair treatment for all citizens; the only way to peace, individually and as a nation, is by obeying the law; persons who break the law must know that they are acting against the will of the majority, and against the safety and peace of the nation.

Now another factor which shaped his life came into force: war.

Santa Anna had been carried into power by the liberal classes, who were against privileges and against the Church's owning and dealing in real property. But, as a rising tide of conservatives made themselves felt, Santa Anna turned his coat and joined the conservatives, taking the army with him. Seeing that this violent change in the government of Mexico could be to their advantage, the American settlers in Texas declared that they wished to be free of Mexican rule. And they were willing to fight for it. Santa Anna led forces against Texas, but after the brutal battle of the Alamo, he was defeated at San Jacinto and made prisoner. To save his own skin, he "ceded" Texas to the rebels, and it became, for a short time, a free republic.

This "Texas War" was very unpopular in Mexico, and when the United States later announced its intention of

annexing the Texas republic (which the legitimate government of Mexico had never recognized as free), Mexico, unprepared, unwisely declared war. Mexico was
poor, and its national honor was to be defended by
blood alone; it lost the war and, in the treaty of peace,
was forced to cede all of California, Arizona, and New
Mexico, as well as Texas, to the United States, for the
sum of $15,000,000.

It must not be supposed that all of Mexico was behind Santa Anna in his prosecution of this war; the
Mexican people and government exiled him three times.
Each time, he somehow made his way back and got
some support.

On the whole, the war was unpopular, and so was
he. The final humiliation of Mexico, in losing so much
of her territory for what was really a paltry sum, was
blamed on him. Juárez, like many other Mexicans,
suffered bitterly at this blow to the national pride and
honor, and like most Mexicans at the time, he blamed
the blundering of Santa Anna for the results and did not
hate the United States for its part in what was seen as
a natural aspiration for expansion to the Pacific Ocean.

During the final years of the war, when Mexico was
in great turmoil, Benito Juárez was named provisional
governor of his native state, Oaxaca.

It might be supposed that this appointment of the
man who, as a boy, had trudged barefoot into the town

to take refuge with his sister, a cook, might seem to be the height of accomplishment. He might well have relaxed, have begun to enjoy his hard-won prestige, to enjoy some luxuries, and to demand recognition and attention. But he did not. His essential character, which changed little throughout the years of his life, was modest, unpretentious, and quiet.

He was, while not spectacular in government, wise and practical. Santa Anna, defeated and on the run, came to Oaxaca to ask for asylum, because Juárez had been one of a group that supported him in the days when he had pretended to be a liberal. Fearing rebellion and civil war in the state if he took in Santa Anna, who was generally hated, Juárez would not accept him. Santa Anna never forgave him for this. Nor did the conservative element among the people, who wanted a leader like Santa Anna—aristocratic and glamorous, supporter of Church privilege—and who despised the "sphinxlike, dark-skinned, upstart Indian" from the Oaxaca hills.

When Juárez's provisional term as governor expired in 1848, he ran for the office and was elected. Upon taking office, he said, "Neither a faction, nor favoritism, nor intrigue, but free and spontaneous choice of the people has placed me in this position." (Juárez did not run for office, with campaigns and speeches, as is the custom in the United States. He merely announced his candidacy and stood on his record.) He went on to say,

"Therefore, no class, or any portion of the citizens, will be oppressed by my government."

Oaxaca was a wealthy state; families like that of Juárez's wife dressed well, had many servants, drove about in fine carriages, and gave brilliant parties, with music and dancing. Yet it is touching to learn that when Juárez was inaugurated as governor of Oaxaca, dozens of Zapotec Indians, from villages like the one he knew in childhood, came down to congratulate him, to bring their loving, pitiful little gifts. He accepted all in quiet courtesy, gave his Zapotec friends the hospitality of his house, and pressed a peso (a lot of money then) into each hand when they said goodbye and started to trudge the long road homeward.

At his second inaugural, he referred to his Indian origin. "A son of the Zapotec people myself, I shall not forget them," he said.

In his efforts to help the Indians, he was practical. First, he thought, they had to be given schools, for he remembered his own desperate struggles to be educated. He set up fifty schools in the state and insisted that there be adequate schooling for girls. He was the first Mexican civil authority to sponsor free public schools for women.

But he knew that the Zapotec and other Indian communities needed more than schools. Their poverty was their basic problem. He hoped to relieve that by giving them roads and an outlet to a port. Thus, they would be able to carry their wool, weaving, leather, and other products to market, and not have to sacrifice them to middlemen at low prices. He ordered that peons who worked the land be exempted from military duty, and each time a new church was consecrated, he saw that a school was inaugurated and blessed at the same time.

Juárez did a number of other practical things while he was governor of Oaxaca. He instituted, and had taught, the rotation of crops. He began work at nine o'clock, so all employees of the state had to do the same, and he would permit no corruption. When he came into office, there was no money in the state coffers. When he left, all the state debts had been paid off. Oaxaca was solvent.

Despite Juárez's deep feeling that no class should be privileged and above the law (the most obvious class being the clergy of the Church, who could be tried only by their own Church courts, not in the civil courts), he recognized that there were good, respectable priests who were fair and honest in their dealing with their flocks.

Even in his last letters, Juárez often says, "If God is willing," and other phrases which indicate that his early religious training remained with him and that he never lost his belief in God or his respect for the spiritual offices of the Church.

It is to be noted that, in dealing with the clergy who worked actively among the people, Juárez was on a firm basis of respect and friendship. In later years, when he attacked top-heavy privilege and Church riches, many thought him to be a kind of devil, an enemy of Christianity. He was an enemy, always, only of what he considered to be unfair privilege, protection, and immunity.

When an epidemic of cholera occurred during his administration, and he and his wife lost their two-year-old daughter, Guadalupe, Juárez walked in procession, with all the people, to pray for divine aid. Though the family of a governor was exempt from the law ordering all burials outside of churches, he himself carried his dead child to the public cemetery, setting an example of obedience to the civil law.

As it might have been . . .

A window in Oaxaca, barred and flush on the street, looks out upon the road which passes the governor's mansion. Two old ladies sit in rockers, knitting, looking out the window at what is going on in the street.

"It has been an hour now since a funeral went by," says one. *"Perhaps the plague is giving way at last."*

"Twenty deaths from cholera last week," answers the other old lady. *"People have been so careless. They should all wear bags of asafetida around their necks and never bathe in hot water. They ask for trouble."*

"Father Melesio hasn't slept more than five hours a night, his housekeeper told me. What with masses for the dead, and last oils, and all the extra confessions, now that people are so scared."

"Look, here comes another funeral!"

Both ladies stop knitting and peer out into the street. Several men are walking quietly along together; they are dressed in black. Just behind them comes a short dark man, hatless, who is carrying a small white coffin on his shoulder. They pace slowly. When the funeral comes abreast of the window, one old lady gasps, "It is the governor! I heard his baby daughter had the cholera. Ay, Jesús, María, y José. The little innocent has flown up to the sky."

"Poor mother. Where is she? I don't see her."

"No. Just men. He made her stay home. He adores her, they say. He is so tender of her, takes such care. But you see, for all his power as governor, he could not save his own child. Man proposes, but God disposes. Who can dispute the will of God?"

"He is a good man, but he doesn't hold much with churches. They are taking the little coffin to the civil cemetery, that's where they are going. And, as governor, he could have his own family buried under the church floor, close to the Blessed Sacrament."

"My son told me that was not to be allowed any more. A new law."

"That explains it, then. The governor is a stickler for law. He loves law like other people love the Blessed Virgin."

"Well, and look where it has got him! Walking by, carrying his own little angel to her grave. And look at him, not a tear, not a sob!"

"Well, he's an Indian. They have no feelings."

"No, that's wrong. They have feelings. They just don't show them. But how that lovely Margarita could have married him . . ."

"Well, see what that marriage got her. She's the gov-

ernor's lady, yes, but there goes her baby. Poor soul."

The funeral has passed by, and the old ladies resume their knitting. Then they suddenly take interest once more; another funeral is coming along the street.

SIX

Exile

In 1852, Juárez's term as governor of Oaxaca came to an end, and he entered private law practice once more. At the same time, he became Director of the Institute of Arts and Sciences and taught civil law there. Thus, he left the realm of politics and administration of the law and became involved again in the actual workings of it in the courts, and in teaching the theory of law.

Though Juárez had enjoyed a period of public trust, respect, and honor, his life soon underwent a sharp change. Santa Anna, to whom he had refused asylum, had returned to the country for the third time and had again seized power, with the help and support of all the conservatives in the country. Juárez was a known liberal who did not believe in the continuation of the entrenched privileges of any class, and Santa Anna considered him not only dangerous but a personal enemy.

Juárez was seized by troops of the new government, held without trial, and eventually exiled from the country. He made his way to Havana, and from there to New Orleans, where he lived for some years in great poverty and distress.

Margarita moved with their children to the little town of Etla, not far from Oaxaca, and started a small general store, selling bolts of cloth, candy, needles and pins, buttons, threads, pots and pans, stationery. She worked hard, having to be on duty much of the time, but she was able to support herself and the children, and even to send her husband a little money once in a while.

Margarita, beautiful, elegant, and aristocratic, never hesitated to help her husband. Despite her distinguished family, she did not run crying to them for help; she rolled up her sleeves and went to work. As she loved her husband, she imitated his qualities of independence and courage.

Juárez was just a poor foreigner in New Orleans. He worked at various odd jobs, to get enough money to pay a modest room rent, eat, and buy books. One of these jobs was in a cigar factory, where he learned to roll tobacco into cigars.

Meanwhile, he read the papers and studied, and dedicated hours to learning all he could about constitutional law. While enduring his exile from his native country and from his family, Juárez continued to study the subject which was his passion all his life, and whenever he could, he attended court trials in New Orleans.

He had the comfort of a few very dear friends who, like himself, longed for an era of law and justice in their own country. Among these were Mata, Ocampo, and Comonfort, names to be associated with Juárez's activities all his life. Among themselves they commented on the fact that Santa Anna, who was the power in control of Mexico, ordered that he be addressed as Serene Highness and Prince President. They could expect no justice for the common man from such an egomaniac. In their exile, these four friends formed a little revolutionary group.

In Mexico, too, there were revolutionary groups who were working toward Santa Anna's defeat. One such group was under the command of General Juan Alvarez, near Acapulco. Finally, Juárez made his way by boat to Acapulco and walked through a tropical rain to Alvarez's camp, arriving drenched and in ruined clothes. Nobody recognized him, and he did not say immediately who he was.

His years of exile had called upon him for the qualities he had learned as a little lad watching over his sheep—patience, vigilance, and steadfastness. Now another of his qualities assumed importance in his life, and indeed, he never lost it. It was tenacity. He was a man who held on, who stuck it out, who did not give up.

As it might have been . . .

At a military camp outside Acapulco, General Juan Alvarez sits in a campaign tent, dictating letters to a secretary, while a torrential tropical rain drums against the tent. The moisture seems to seep through the canvas and fall in a fine mist on the general, in his military uniform. He is an imposing man, with white hair springing up off a high forehead, strong black arched brows above his hooded dark eyes, a long nose, and a stern mouth fringed by a drooping dark mustache. Erect and immaculate, he looks up with some annoyance as the flap of his tent is held back, and his son Diego enters with an undistinguished-looking man whose clothes, shabby and patched to begin with, have been plastered to his body by the storm. As he steps forward modestly to speak to the resplendent rebel general, his old shoes squelch with water at each step. His black hair is flat against his head and dripping onto his face.

Diego salutes briskly. "A new recruit for our cause, Father."

Then the stranger says steadily, "I heard that men were fighting for freedom here. I have come to join you."

The general accepts him with a curt nod. "Get this man some dry clothes," he orders.

An orderly appears, after a short wait, with a dry pair of cotton trousers and a blanket. Nothing more.

"We haven't any other stores of clothing," *is the apologetic explanation.*

The man bows his thanks. "I am grateful for these," *he says.* "In my youth, I wore little else." *He smiles suddenly, the white teeth flashing in the dark face with a look of merriment.*

Comfortably dry, barefoot, relieved of the squashy shoes, he becomes serious again.

"I can serve as secretary, if you wish."

"Can you write?" *General Alvarez stares at him keenly.*

"Yes. Very well."

"Where did you learn?"

"In Oaxaca. I am a lawyer."

"Oh? Your name, please?"

"Benito Juárez."

General Alvarez stares. "The governor?"

"I was governor. Now I am a simple recruit, here to fight for freedom."

The general stands up and extends his hand. Juárez takes it solemnly.

"Welcome, licenciado. We are glad to have you with us."

SEVEN

The First Congress

Sᴀɴᴛᴀ ᴀɴɴᴀ, who had three times seized power, could not hold it any longer. The revolutionary forces around the country, which were against him, drove him out. General Juan Alvarez marched to Cuernavaca from Acapulco, with Comonfort and Juárez, and there they met with the other friends of Juárez who had shared his exile, Ocampo and Mata. They set up a provisional government; Comonfort was delegated power to rule, and he appointed a cabinet. Juárez was given the post of Minister of Justice and Public Education.

Now, this was very much a revolutionary government, which had not yet received the vote of the people themselves; until then, its officers could not feel that they had the confidence of the majority.

The four friends who had starved and plotted in New Orleans then came together and drafted a plan, or a

statement of what they stood for, which they promulgated, and which was made public, so that all Mexicans
could think it over. This was called the Plan of Ayutla,
so named from the town in which it was launched.

The Plan of Ayutla proclaimed the downfall of Santa
Anna and demanded that a constitutional congress be
convened, to draft laws that would guarantee to the
people their natural rights and that would prevent another dictator from seizing power.

The plan attracted many thinking men, but the invasion of the capital by General Alvarez, with his savage
soldiers, changed their minds again, for the troops committed many crimes and brought disorder to the city.
Comonfort, temporarily titled president, who had been
advising Alvarez, lost power. Just before Comonfort
gave up and left the capital, Juárez managed to place
before the congress a law he had drafted as Minister of
Justice. This law did away with two immunities against
trial in public courts. These immunities were called
fueros, and they were enjoyed by members of the clergy
and the army. They provided that no priest or soldier
could be tried for any crime by the civil courts, but only
by his own courts—a privilege that Juárez always fought
as being most unfair.

Juárez managed to see his law voted in, to take its
place as part of the law of the land, known as Ley
Juárez, or Juárez's Law. Naturally, the law and Juárez

were bitterly hated by the groups that had lost their advantages.

Then Comonfort left the capital, Alvarez resigned, and a more moderate government took over. This government appreciated Juárez, and he was returned to his native state as governor. He had not been long away from the capital when he learned that another principle he believed in with all his heart and mind had been formulated into law. This was the Lerdo Law, named for Lerdo de Tejada, who drafted it. This law took away Church lands which were lying useless and uncultivated and returned them to the people. Church lands were called mortmain, or the dead hand, because, belonging to the Church, they never changed owners.

Having had firsthand experience with politics, with the manner in which authorities yielded to pressure and compromised on issues in order to remain in power, Juárez gradually transferred his loyalty to the congress. It seemed to him that men, taken singly, were likely to give in to pressure, whereas a congress, after all, consisted of many men, and a balance could be kept. In this, he was a true democrat, for he always suspected the weakness of single men and never believed that any one single person should govern a people.

Here he was proven right, time after time, when even his dearest friends, despite his steady loyalty to them, betrayed him. But that came later, when the country was in the throes of a war to expel the French from Mexico.

While Juárez was governor of Oaxaca, he instituted changes which confirmed his modesty and his dislike of personal display. "Speaking of bad habits," he wrote, "former governors often followed the custom of having armed guards in their homes, and of wearing special dress. As soon as I assumed power [as governor], I abolished this custom, using the hat and dress of an ordinary citizen, and living in my home without military guard or display of any kind, since I believe that the respectability of a ruler derives from the law and right conduct and not from costumes and martial accessories proper only for stage kings."

Nowadays, we feel that Juárez's modest conduct was the only proper behavior, but in his day it was a great break with tradition, really startling and almost scandalous.

An outstanding characteristic of Juárez was that he believed in looking ahead and in preparing for trouble. No doubt this was part of his childhood training, as he pastured his sheep; the shepherd must always feel the storm coming and get his sheep safely home.

Juárez had seen many liberal laws passed by the constitutional congress, many privileged classes deprived of their unfair powers, and other reforms passed into law. But, as he could observe with sorrow, having a law written into the books did not mean that the people would obey it. There were strong currents of opposition to the reform laws precisely from the groups of people who stood to lose their advantages through them.

First, the Church. Catholics (all Mexicans were Catholic, and are to this day, except perhaps 4 or 5 percent of the people) were forbidden to swear allegiance to the constitution. In other words, they were urged to rebel, and by an authority they had all been taught to obey. Many obeyed. Also, the military were restless and might join irritated and rebellious conservatives at any time.

Juárez saw these troubles taking shape, and his answer was quietly to strengthen his state, to put the laws into effect, and to get Oaxaca on an even keel financially, while making all the reforms he could, as well as building roads and schools.

Then his friend Comonfort was elected president in 1857, and Juárez was elected president of the Supreme Court. The law provided that should the president die or leave office for any reason during his term, the president of the Supreme Court would succeed him as president. (There is no vice-president in Mexico.) Juárez then returned to the capital with his family, knowing that he was to act and live "in the eye of the storm," but confident that he had left his native state well organized and strongly administered.

As it might have been . . .

An old-fashioned dressing room. There are sconces for candles on each side of a large shaving mirror, where a man in dark trousers and white shirt is shaving with an old-fashioned, long-blade razor. Half his face is covered with foam from his shaving mug. To one side is a tall chest of drawers, with a comb and brush, a watch, and a handkerchief on top. Over a chair is draped a high white starched collar and a black necktie. A half-open door shows a glimpse of a bedroom, also furnished with heavy old-fashioned chairs, dressing tables, and a wide bed with a white coverlet.

A pretty woman, plump, dark-eyed, and with softly curling dark brown hair appears in the doorway. She wears a simple dark-blue dress.

"Nito, the man is here to take your measurements."

He puts down his razor and turns to her inquiringly.
"What man? Did you send for him?"

"No. He says all the governors are measured for their gala uniforms, for state affairs."

The man turns calmly back to his mirror and continues shaving a moment, while the woman waits, uncertain, in the doorway. Then he stops, pats his face dry with a towel, and wipes his razor clean.

"Give him this money for his trouble in coming. But

I am not to be measured." At her look of inquiry, he continues, "Because I do not intend to wear any gala uniform, ever."

He goes to her, pats her cheek affectionately. "You, my love, may have all the pretty dresses I can afford. And I like you in deep garnet red. But I am a simple man of the people and I will never put on any trappings of superiority at all. I will wear quiet dark suits, spotless linen. Tell the uniform tailor. And the hatter. There'll be a hatter, too, I suppose, ready to make me a big hat with feathers. Can't you see me in one? I would feel like a fool. No, mi amor. A governor, or any other person elected to a place of respect in the government, should earn that respect by honesty, hard work, and regard for the good of the people. The brilliant uniforms have nothing to do with it."

EIGHT

The Capital in Veracruz

As PRESIDENT of the Supreme Court, the Indian boy from the hills had reached what must have seemed to him the pinnacle of success. His whole devotion was to law, and now he occupied the post that represented the highest dignity of the law. He resolved to act always with justice, fairness, and good will.

But already one of his trusted friends had begun to waver. Comonfort began to give in to pressure groups who advised him to assume dictatorial powers and to soften some of the liberal laws of the constitution. He called Juárez in to discuss these ideas. Juárez answered, "I wish you joy in the course you are taking, but I will not join you."

Nevertheless, he did not betray Comonfort, the president. He said nothing and waited.

Comonfort and soldiers took the palace, and the con-

spiracy to seize greater power was achieved. Juárez was
made prisoner and kept in the palace, under guard, for
three weeks. The conspiracy demanded that the Ley
Lerdo and the Ley Juárez be repealed; Comonfort was
willing to do this, but Juárez refused. At last Comonfort
lost support and voluntarily went into exile. Thus,
Juárez became president for the rest of the term, according to the constitution. However, the conspiracy
was not willing to recognize Juárez, the legal president,
and they pursued him, intending to capture and im-
prison him again. He got away, walking across fields at
night, catching mail coaches, and struggling along
through the countryside, helped and fed by the country
people who were loyal. He managed to get to the city
of Guanajuato, where he declared to the nation that he
was the legal president and that he would remain in
office.

Luckily, there were a number of governors of states
who stood by Juárez and the constitution. They had
some military power, which they pooled in a sort of
league, and Juárez had the help of two liberal friends,
Ocampo and Prieto, who had been with him in New
Orleans, to help form his cabinet.

But being legally right was not enough. The forces of
the league were defeated in a battle, and Juárez and his
friends were caught in the city of Guadalajara, at the
mercy of their enemies. Through the oratory and cour-

age of Prieto, who addressed the soldiers ready to shoot him and Juárez, peace talks were arranged. Now all Mexico began to appreciate the strong character of Juárez, who had acted with steady courage throughout all these trials.

The conservative forces were strong, and they began to conquer central Mexico. Juárez and his friends fled; they made their way to the coast and took ship. They went to Panama, and then, after crossing the isthmus, they came by small boat to Veracruz, where they disembarked and set up their government.

It was difficult indeed, without funds and without a personal army, to set up the only government they could consider *legal,* in a coastal city, far away from the power and excitement of the capital. But Juárez counted on the good sense of the Mexican people, and knew, with certainty, that they would eventually rally to the cause of legality, of law and the constitution, having seen enough of dictators.

Meanwhile, back in Oaxaca, where she had gone with her children, Juárez's wife learned that certain of the vindictive conservatives intended to kidnap her and her children. With remarkable courage, she simply took her children and walked all the way to Veracruz, to join her husband. The way was not easy, over high mountains and frightening gorges. We have no first-

hand record of the journey she made, with her little
daughters, Mañuela, Felicitas, and Margarita; nevertheless, one can reconstruct much of the whole adventure. Señora Juárez was fleeing for her life and the lives
of her children. She was terrified, but determined somehow to reach her husband. His presence always meant
safety and peace to her. She dared not be seen in daylight. Juárez's own people, the Zapotec Indians of the
mountains, who lived in small villages and on tiny
rancherías, hid her and her little ones by day, and
guided them by night. The tropical rains were falling
and the mountain paths were treacherous with mud.
Once, we know, Doña Margarita slipped and would
have fallen, perhaps to her death, if her hoop skirt had
not caught on a bush and held her until she could be
rescued. Hiding during the day, sharing the poor bowls
of beans and tortillas offered by kindly people who
wanted to help her and who endangered their lives in
doing so, she struggled on, and at last she got to
Veracruz. Juárez was comforted and strengthened by
having his family with him again.

Many of the conservatives called him names like
"Devil" and "Horrible Indian." Juárez had not been a
man who had a warm and loving following, even from
the men who believed, as he did, in free and liberal
laws. They respected him, but there were very few

endearing anecdotes about him, few stories to reflect some charming quality. He was admired for rectitude, for dignity, and for his courage.

But in Veracruz a story circulated which began to draw people to him, not because of his intellectual qualities, but because it revealed him as humble and a man of the people.

He had moved into a house in Veracruz with his cabinet. They had entered at night, and the owner of the house had not had a look at the president, Benito Juárez. The next morning, he went out to find her and asked her to draw some water for him. "Draw it yourself," she ordered him, believing him to be a servant. He quietly did so. Later, when she learned that the man she had ordered about was the president, she was very much upset, but the story made the rounds of people all over Mexico, and at last people began to love their indomitable little Indian president, who never felt himself to be too grand to do the work of a servant.

Mexico was going to need his patience, his tenacity, his courage, and his optimism in the years to come, for events were building up which were to challenge all the ideals he had striven for and to tear down all his hopes.

As it might have been . . .

A poor Indian's hut in the mountains of Oaxaca. Night has fallen, and the family, consisting of a middle-aged man, a woman, and two small children, is sitting eating. They are squatting near a fire, where the woman is toasting tortillas and filling them with beans from a pot. As she rolls each tortilla and passes them to her husband, then to her children, each says, "Gracias, Mamá." The half-open door of the hut shows only dark country-side and a sky in which the stars are shining. Suddenly a little dog outside begins a frantic barking; the man jumps up at once. Someone is coming. He goes to the door just as a woman dressed in dark clothes and a long cape comes to stand there. Neither can see the other, but when the lady speaks, it is evident that she is an educated woman from the city.

"I beg you to help me, good people . . ." *She stands, waveringly, in the doorway. The dog has ceased to bark so shrilly as his master says,* "Come in. You are welcome."

As she steps in, the woman of the hut lights a small candle, and Margarita Maza de Juárez is revealed. With her, clinging to her skirts, white-faced, scared, and tired, are three little girls, the oldest about five.

"Be seated. Warm yourself," *says the Indian hesi-*

*tantly, for Spanish is not his language, though he knows
a few words.*

"We are in trouble, my little ones and I," says the
lady. "My husband has told me that if ever we need
help, we are to come to his people. So I have come. I
am Margarita Juárez."

*The Indian bows and nods respectfully. "You are the
señora of Don Benito, the good governor."*

"And these are his children. We came, hidden in a
covered cart, so that no one could see us. We have
nothing with us, but I have some money. I cannot pay
for your help, but I can share the cost of your food and
the warmth of your fire."

"What has happened that you come to us, so frightened?"

"My husband awaits us in Veracruz. But his enemies
have threatened to kidnap us . . . me and the children
. . . to hold us, so as to make him suffer and force him
to do as they will. He is the president, you know, but
there are many who hate him because he defends the
poor."

"I know."

*There is a long silence. One of the children offers his
tortilla to the smallest Juárez daughter. She accepts it
shyly, murmuring, "Gracias."*

"Doña Margarita, you will sleep here in our humble
home. You will be safe here."

"*I want to get to Veracruz. Can't we walk . . . over the mountain?*"

Again, a long silence. Then the man speaks, "We will guide you, Doña Margarita. We will guide you and defend you. Rest now, and have no fear."

NINE

The Reform Laws

THE PRESIDENT in Veracruz had no funds with which to support his government. A civil war was raging between the conservative forces, which had a considerable army and a professional soldier to command it, General Miguel Miramón, and Juárez's legal government, which also had an army, under an equally gifted man, General Santos Degollado.

Besides lack of funds to carry on the struggle and to try to secure peace, so as to take over the government to which Juárez knew himself to be legally entitled, there was bitterness about money owed to foreign governments. Some of this debt had been legally contracted, through loans; part of the money was owed to private persons and to companies which had been investing in Mexico under promises from the government that their money would be safe.

60.

This matter of indebtedness to the United States, England, France, and Spain made relations between the governments very difficult, especially as France did not want to see Spain get power and influence in Mexico, Spain did not want France to secure power and influence, England wanted to make sure France was kept out, and the United States did not want *any* European power to come into its neighboring country by force of arms and, pretending to collect debts, take over a position of dangerous power on its very doorstep.

Thus, there were all sorts of threats and troubles hanging over Juárez's legal government, and at the same time, the powerful conservative group was willing to bargain with the Europeans or Americans to expel him. Considering this background of violence, intrigue, and greed, it is astounding that Juárez could hang on with the patience and equanimity he showed.

After careful thought, Juárez finally decided upon his course of action. In order to get funds to fight off the rebellious conservatives, and to affirm his position, he promulgated and announced to the country a series of laws that came to be known as the Reform Laws.

First, he nationalized Church property. This meant that the government would be in a position to sell much of the valuable property that was held by the Church. The government could get funds in this way, and the land could go back into production for the nation.

Second, he declared the official separation of Church and state. (This is a principle of law which has been acknowledged in all the democracies of the Western world, but in those times, it was a bold and modern step to take.) Of course this move aroused the passionate opposition of the Church.

Third, he established a civil registry to keep records of births, deaths, and marriages. (Formerly, this had been an exclusive right and duty of the Church.)

Fourth, he secularized the cemeteries. (This upset many of the humble people of the country, who had a great terror of not being buried in hallowed or blessed ground.)

There were other laws, as well, all of them tending to place Mexico in line with other enlightened and progressive countries of the West.

Juárez's proclamations of civil power startled and frightened many people. But the conservatives had just done something which swung much popular sentiment over to Juárez's side. One of the conservative generals under Miramón, a man named Marquez, had captured the town of Tacubaya, just outside Mexico City (now part of the city), which had resisted him. He then ordered the slaughter of all the prisoners in the jails, the sick and wounded in the hospital, as well as the nurses and doctors. This atrocity made many people take a different point of view about the kind of government they wanted.

Juárez stood by the Reform Laws he had promulgated, and asserted to the country and to all the diplomats who had access to him that there must be complete freedom of civil power and complete religious liberty in the country.

One asks, since Juárez was so deeply a man of law, how he could feel justified in simply promulgating decrees while still only a provisional president and before he had assured his place by election. Juárez had thought for a year about this matter, and he had finally seen it as necessary, in order to give his movement a strong reason for being. He intended to have the laws ratified by the congress, if ever he could win enough peace and control to call a congress again.

His Reform Laws had one strong, necessary aim: to secularize society—that is, to free it from dictation by the Church, which, in Juárez's view, should hold spiritual power only and should not rule the people or hold property. Having promulgated his explosive laws, and having declared the intentions of his government, he sat still to see what would happen.

The whole country was in turmoil. The United States had never given up thinking of Mexico as a backward country that needed its own firm hand in guidance, and the United States also coveted not only parts of the north of Mexico and lower California (offering to buy the latter) but also the narrow Isthmus of Tehuantepec, where, it was often thought, a second canal could be built to connect the Pacific Ocean with the Caribbean and thus with the Atlantic.

It was always Juárez's way to let things develop, to give people and events "enough rope," as the saying goes, to reveal their true character. Thus, he permitted negotiations to go on for a long time between an American diplomat named Allan McLane and his own friend and representative Ocampo. These two finally worked out a treaty which would have permitted the building of a canal across the isthmus and the policing of it by American troops. The only thing Juárez had insisted upon, in discussions with Ocampo, was that Mexican territorial sovereignty be rigidly protected.

There was an outcry in the press against the treaty, and the American Congress would not accept it anyhow, so the whole thing died out, without Juárez having to take a public stand either for or against it. Yet his enemies used the idea of the treaty (which many people had not studied at all) to attempt to break down his reputation. Actually, he said and wrote, on many occasions, that he would never, under any circumstances, compromise Mexican territory, or give away or sell one inch of it.

The American Congress refused to accept the proposed treaty because of the struggle for power going on between the North and the "slave states"; the North thought the treaty would open up territory so that settlers could go into Mexico, later rebel, and demand freedom (as Texas did), and then form slave states.

So, here was Juárez, a president living away from the capital, in simple rooms, without money, opposed by a strong army and by people who hated everything he was striving for. He must have been a deeply troubled man, though all his letters and his constant attitude was one of optimism. He believed strongly that someday Mexico would have a body of governing law that did away with privilege and guaranteed every citizen the same rights; stronger even than that belief was his habit of endurance. As his enemies became more aware of his qualities, the very strength of his position of unaltering, calm endurance became a weapon.

The opposition—conservatives and the Church, plus a large segment of the army—was now ready to take an extreme step. They were ready to bring in a new government, under force of foreign arms.

As it might have been . . .

Veracruz. A simple, poor room with white-washed walls, a deep window with bars across it. It is hot and muggy. At a plain, unpainted table, in a straight chair, a man is sitting, working. His swarthy forehead glistens with sweat; his black hair is plastered to his head like a cap. He is wearing black trousers and a white shirt, which is wrinkled and damp from perspiration. On the table are paper, an ink pot, and a pen, and there are several law books. There is also a pitcher of water, covered with a napkin, because a few flies are buzzing lazily about. The man's black coat and white scarf hang on the back of his chair.

A young man, evidently a clerk, enters hastily, and the man working at the table looks up.

"Señor Presidente, the mail has come." *A bundle of letters and papers and a few official-appearing documents are laid on the table.*

"Thank you."

"I will be in the next room if you wish to dictate, or to have any messages taken to the telegraph." *The young man's excitement becomes apparent to the man working.*

"What has happened, Juan? What did you want to tell me?"

"*Rumors are that the liberal army is gaining, Señor Presidente!*"

"*Sometimes rumors turn out to be true, and sometimes not.*" *Juárez smiles faintly.*

"*But if they are true, we will be going back to Mexico City, won't we?*"

"*We will, never fear. In time. Remember, Juan, it is wise to treat time as a friend, never an enemy. When time is your friend, all good things come to pass.*"

"*Oh, but, Señor Presidente, time . . . I don't want to get old!*"

Juárez smiles broadly. "*But you will, Juan. We all will. Someday remember what I have told you. Time can be your friend. Now leave me. I still have work to do.*"

"*You have not eaten anything, and it is already four in the afternoon.*"

"*I must finish this. Thank you, Juan.*"

The smile has disappeared. Juan is dismissed.

TEN

Civil War

THE EXCUSE for tempting a foreign nobleman over the seas to assume a throne in Mexico was the fact that the Mexican government could not pay its debts and had declared itself unable to do so for an indefinite period.

Who was the foreign prince? He was the Archduke Maximilian of Austria, brother of the Emperor Franz Josef. This young man had been educated with the idea that he was born to rule something, somewhere. The old theory of the divine right of kings had died out, but the few surviving royal families in Europe were taught that they were born to rule the lower classes, and to demonstrate to them the ideals of education, elegance, and nobility. A country must be found for every prince to rule. Some time had been spent trying to find such a country for Maximilian and his ambitious wife, Carlota. When finally, through the scheming of the French emperor Napoleon III, Mexico was offered to Maximilian, the archduke persuaded himself that the Mexican people had sent for him, as for a sort of savior.

Actually, the machinations of Napoleon III, the Spanish government, and the English were carried out in order to try to give a protective coating of legality to what they planned to do: hurriedly sack the country of money (through customs duties and taxes) and pay themselves back for money previously loaned, either through government offices or through private banks and business enterprises, which were demanding their money back. Since many French citizens, and others, had money invested in the Mexican companies, they were willing to accept the idea of a French-protected government, which would wrench their funds back from that savage, faraway country, Mexico.

Within Mexico, a hastily convened group of landowners, churchmen, and military leaders gave the appearance of "sending" for the foreign prince. And well-to-do people, romantic ladies who had heard of the handsome, golden-bearded archduke and his beautiful wife, dreamed of the glamor of a royal court in Mexico, and of being able to live comfortably within their privileged circles, unworried by rebellion from the tattered, dirty, and ignorant peons, who should learn their place and get back to their work in the fields and mines.

It must be remembered that these were the educated people, the washed, the solid citizens, who were quite willing to be kind and charitable to the poor but who felt reluctant to associate with them on terms of equality. The French Revolution, with its cry of "Liberty, equality, and fraternity," had given way to rule by a cruel rabble, and France itself, a country Mexicans had always admired as a leader in Europe, had returned to government by an emperor, Napoleon III.

Juárez must have felt himself, and his liberal government, in a position of extreme peril. French, English, and Spanish warships menaced from the sea, and the imposition of the archduke was to take place, backed by a strong French army which would come in from the sea and land at Veracruz. With his own liberal troops under Degollado fighting in the north, and in expectation of the French landing at Veracruz, Juárez was cornered.

Still without funds, Juárez's general Degollado then swooped down upon a British armed consignment of money going to England and robbed it. Hard up as he was, Juárez could not countenance this, for his mind cleaved to the law, and he saw things either as right, and therefore legal, or wrong, and therefore criminal.

He ordered the stolen money returned, and the officers who had led the attack on the British mule train punished.

Degollado reluctantly gave the British back their money, and then entered into negotiations with the British minister in Mexico, George Mathew, who convinced Degollado to try to persuade Juárez to try for a "negotiated peace." This negotiated peace depended on the British acting as mediators between the liberals and the conservatives. Juárez was urged to give up his presidency and let the negotiators fix up a sort of compromise.

Juárez was not a vain man, but he had to make it clear that he remained president not merely because he wanted the power and dignity of that position. He wrote to Mathew as follows: "If the war had a personal object, that is, if the question were whether I were to remain in power or not, the decent and dignified course would be for me to retire from the post I occupy . . ." But he went on to make it clear that this was not the case. "I remain at my post as a matter of duty and with the noble object of cooperating in the conquest of peace for my country. And I hold the profound conviction that peace will be stable and lasting when the general will, *expressed through law*, reforms the constitution and appoints and removes rulers, and not an audacious minority."

To Degollado he was very forbearing. He wrote him:
"I in no wise approve your plan of pacification, and on
the contrary, in fulfillment of my duty, I shall employ
every legal means in my power to oppose it." But he
signed himself, "I repeat that I am your friend, Benito
Juárez."

As Degollado persisted in a plan to make a separate
peace, Juárez ordered him to Veracruz to stand trial for
robbing the British goods train. Later Juárez suspended
the trial. Meanwhile, his liberal forces under General
González Ortega began gaining victories, and many
faint hearts returned to the liberal side and to Juárez,
the personification of a cause . . . a steady, firm, un-
corruptible figure.

In the meantime, the whole matter of the Treaty of
McLane-Ocampo was dragging on. Juárez, like other
liberals, hoped somehow to get a loan from the United
States, enough to carry on the war and throw out the
rebels, if possible, before the French-protected Maximilian arrived to take over the "throne" of Mexico.

The American Congress did not want to ratify the
treaty because of the fear of Southern slave states moving into Mexican territory and overbalancing the power
of the North. Moreover, there had been constant opposition to the treaty in Mexico. At last it became clear
who opposed it: Juárez himself. He had allowed the
negotiations to go along because no legal point was

involved until ratification became necessary—and because it was good for England, Spain, and France to
know that some negotiations were going on between
Juárez's government and the United States. Juárez accomplished one thing by his patience: the United States
recognized his government as the legal government of
Mexico. This accomplished, the treaty itself, with its
dangerous mention of foreign troops on Mexican soil,
could be set aside.

Things seemed to be working out well, at last, for the
hard-pressed and brave government of Juárez and his
liberal cabinet. General Miramón and his conservative
army were defeated, and on Christmas Day, the tri-
umphant liberal army entered Mexico City.

News traveled slowly in those difficult days, and
President Juárez was in attendance at an opera, with
his family, in Veracruz when he got word of the victory of his own forces. There was a full house; the
company was presenting the French opera *Les Hugue-
nots*, which is about the religious wars in France. A
courier was admitted to the president's box. Then the
president rose. The conductor of the orchestra demanded silence by rapping his baton, and the whole
house listened as Juárez read a bulletin announcing the
triumph of the liberal cause. The civil war in Mexico
was over.

After a moment's startled silence, the whole audience

rose to its feet, acclaiming the man who had stood firm and unmoving through all the dangers and troubles, believing he would be sure to triumph in the end. The opera singers burst into "La Marseillaise," and there was a frantic scene of celebration.

Juárez took it soberly. Perhaps he wondered how the capital, stronghold of the conservative forces, would receive him when he returned there. He need not have worried. The capital celebrated for eight hours when, at last, Juárez drove into the city in his usual modest black carriage.

He was happy. But he was still solemn and quiet. He knew that while military opposition had been overcome, there were still problems to face, many of them extremely dangerous and difficult to solve.

Still, as was his way, he went forward slowly and carefully, making no move until he had thought everything through, until he had examined all the legal aspects, and until he had decided where his duty lay.

As it might have been . . .

On a balcony over a street in Mexico City, two pretty young girls are waiting for a procession to pass by. It is a cold January day, and they are wrapped in warm, bright-colored, woolen rebozos. They are sitting on little chairs, and between them, on another chair, is a tray of many-colored paper flowers that they have made. As they sit, their busy fingers are twisting and wiring and bending crepe paper and fastening it into place, making other blossoms.

"There will be fireworks tonight, and a band concert, and a big ball as well, Mama says. Don't you wish we could go to the ball, Carmela?"

"Well, it will be enough to see the fireworks and hear the music. Only the rich people will go to the ball, I suppose."

"The rich people? Oh no. They won't go. They don't like him. Still, some of them may go, to curry favor, you know. Papa says people will change their coats twenty times a day if it means money in the purse, or even beans in the pot!"

"I suppose so." The older girl is more serious.

"The paper said there were fiestas all along the rail-way line from Veracruz, at every stop! Mexico City will go crazy!"

"I for one will be glad to have a president in residence here again. It makes me feel safer, somehow."

"Look, here they come! But it isn't brilliant at all," cries the younger girl in disappointment. "There are the soldiers, the escorts on their horses, but it is just a plain black carriage. Shall we throw our flowers, after all?"

"Well . . ." The other girl is hesitant.

The carriage rolls by slowly. Inside, one can glimpse President Juárez, dignified, quiet, making no attempt to respond to the crowds that are yelling, "Viva!"

The girls toss a few of their bright paper flowers. One falls on top of the carriage, and then rolls off and is crushed in the street, as crowds follow the carriage, shouting and singing.

"Anyhow," says the younger one, "we can see the fireworks tonight from this balcony. Anyhow . . ."

ELEVEN

The Suspension of Payments

T HE FIRST acts Juárez carried out clearly showed that he meant to enforce the laws which he had written into the constitution, especially as to freedom of religion and as to the right of the government to sell Church property.

Because there were many financial problems facing his government, Juárez had hoped that the sale of the former Church property would provide some funds. But matters stronger than law intervened here. Catholics had been forbidden by their Church to buy or sell any of the condemned property, under pain of excommunication. Excommunication is a dreadful, a desperate, prospect for a believing Catholic, and so the faithful would not have anything to do with Church property, even though they felt glad the civil war was over and were willing to be loyal to their government and to Juárez.

Besides, the Church property had been plundered by thieves and was far less rich than had been supposed.

The government then faced up to the following debts:

There was an extensive foreign debt, which was being paid off through customs duties. Not a cent of these duties reached the national treasury.

There were dividends on the national debt to pay.

The army had to be paid, for it had bled and fought for months on the mere promise of payment.

The separate Mexican states owed the federal treasury much money, but were unable to pay it.

Besides this, there was a national debt that had been acquired in a strange way. A Swiss financial company, Jecker, had floated bonds to pay the soldiers who opposed Juárez in the conservative army. But the conservatives lost and the Jecker bank failed. Meanwhile, France, through citizens who had bought the bonds, held a claim against the Mexican government (now Juárez's government) for the bonds, to the extent of eighty-six million francs. The French government, through its diplomatic representatives in Mexico, was determined to get this money back.

Juárez's government made frantic efforts to float loans outside the country, which meant, of course, the United States, since Europe was lined up against Mexico. Juárez drastically cut his own salary and those of his cabinet members. It was not enough.

The United States was suddenly embroiled in a civil war of its own and could not take active steps to help Mexico, beyond continuing to recognize Juárez's government as the legal one, even after French arms had brought the flamboyant court to Mexico City and Archduke Maximilian had been declared "Emperor of Mexico."

The imposition of the emperor came about because Juárez, at a loss to find any other legal way to get money enough to run the government, declared a moratorium on the foreign debts. That is, he declared Mexico unable to pay its debts, and he advised the countries that they would have to wait indefinitely for their payment.

Meanwhile, there were other troubles awaiting Juárez. General Ortega, who had been willing to make peace with the conservatives, partly giving in to them, was elected president of the Supreme Court, and was therefore due to succeed to the presidency if anything happened to Juárez. At once he got up a petition to ask Juárez to resign, which would have left the way clear for him to become president. Juárez would not do this, and when the matter was put to a vote in the congress, Juárez won by a small majority.

Curiously enough, the reason for Ortega's opposition to Juárez was Juárez's rigid adherence to law. His opponents objected to his stanch support of the law at every turn, and they cried against him, in the words of St. Paul, "The letter of the law kills."

But Juárez held to the law as the one protection for all citizens, the one method of assuring order, peace, and justice, and of preventing the greed of one class from doing damage to another. Ortega, a military man, wanted to bend and adjust the law, so as to give the president power to make peace as he saw fit. As a civilian, Juárez felt he must defend the country's constitution against everything, and therefore he meant to oppose any enemy.

Meanwhile, the Spanish had landed armies in Veracruz and were getting ready to fight their way to the capital.

Due to this emergency, the conservatives rallied behind Juárez's government, and the congress allowed him some extraordinary powers. Juárez ordered Veracruz evacuated, and the Spanish found themselves in a city without food or services. Then Juárez issued a statement:

"Let the defenseless enemy, to whom we have given generous hospitality, live tranquil and secure under the protection of our laws. Let us defend ourselves against this war to which we are provoked by strictly observing the law and usages established for the benefit of humanity."

He also announced that all legitimate grievances would be duly heard and settled according to law. The Spaniards and the English, who had been pressing claims, became very cooperative and were willing to negotiate. Only the French minister was adamant. A French army landed at Veracruz, and it became clear to Mexicans that this was a very serious threat.

The French marched on the rich city of Puebla, but there they were defeated resoundingly in a battle on May 5, which the Mexicans still celebrate as a national holiday.

This defeat only made the French more determined, and information was sent to Juárez by Mexicans in Paris that a great expeditionary force was being raised and equipped in France and would sail for Mexico soon. Juárez's answer was short and characteristic: "There is no help but defense. The Mexican people are resolved upon it, and their government will employ every means permitted by international law, for self-defense."

It is clear that Juárez's conception of law was not narrow and applicable only to his own country and people. He was devoted to every system of law, *national and international,* which set down rules for fair, just, and humane behavior of one human being toward another.

Not long before, one of his ministers had made out a list of judicial costs and had sent it to be published.

When Juárez heard of this, he countermanded the publication at once, because the constitution guarantees *free* trial to all.

Just as he acted to defend his own constitution, he ordered his generals and the troops who were fighting against the invading French to observe international law. He would have no looting, no mistreatment of civilians, and no torture of prisoners. He was not always obeyed, but his attitude was clear and it never changed.

Now the French, under new generals, and with fresh troops, set siege to Puebla once more. The city was defended with great courage, but after three months it fell, and the French saw the road to Mexico City open.

When Juárez received this news, he was dejected, but in the crisis, he was practical and thought far ahead. He did not intend to give up, but he would not subject the capital to the cruelty of a long siege. He thought the country as a whole must be defended, and one way to do that was to make sure that its legitimate government was never taken prisoner. Accordingly, he quietly made plans to leave the city. The Mexican colors were taken down from the government palace, the flag was given to Juárez, he kissed it, shouted "Viva Mexico!" and went inside. Shortly afterward, his coach rolled out of the city, and the government was gone.

As it might have been . . .

The scene is a lonely road leading north from Mexico City. A signpost in battered letters, with an arrow, proclaims: FROM MEXICO CITY, 100 KMS. TO TEQUISQUIAPAN, 80 KMS. *The sign is blurred by a great cloud of dust which comes swiftly along the road, enveloping a black carriage, pulled by two horses. It stops in front of the sign. The horses are tired; they stand with drooping heads. A man leans out of the carriage to speak to the driver.*

"No need to hurry now, driver. Spare the beasts."

There is a sound of agreement from the driver. He flicks his whip gently, the horses start up again, but now they proceed at a slower pace, though the road is flat.

The dust forms again around the carriage and accompanies it as it disappears down the road.

Soon there is nothing but the countryside again. It is dusty and dry, with a tree seen only here and there. In the distance ahead is a pale-blue line of mountains. There are a few clumps of cactus, with paddle-shaped leaves.

It is lonely and silent.

The president of Mexico has just passed by.

TWELVE

Maximilian Arrives

THERE FOLLOWED the long, hard, and bloody war to rid Mexico of a foreign empire which was set up, under French arms, because the French and other European countries wanted to have a government which would serve their interests and devise means for them to get back their loans and investments.

Mixed into this economic wish, which was the most important one, were two misconceptions about Mexico and the New World. The first was the idea that Mexico was a country of primitive savages who should be governed for their own good and taught European ways. The second was that Mexicans wanted to be governed by outsiders, and that they would like the idea of a monarchy.

In some ways, there was reason to believe the latter of these two basically wrong ideas. It is true that Agustín

Iturbide, one of the first great rebels against Spain, who had taken over the government after Mexico gained her independence in 1820, had declared himself an emperor almost at once, seeming to indicate that the Mexicans liked the idea of empire. Also, Santa Anna, who came later, and who was elected president under a liberal party, soon wanted to be called "Your Serene Highness." These two gentlemen did their countrymen no favor, in their foolish vanity, making it seem natural that all Mexicans would wish to have royalty on a throne as their government.

Another attitude that must be taken into consideration is that playing kings and queens, princes and princesses, has always been a diversion of childhood, and some people never grow up. To many romantic Mexicans, the idea of a court, of elaborate etiquette, costumes, and crowns, seemed romantic and enticing.

Then, too, the country had been in a chaotic condition and continually at war for many long years, and some practical people thought, We have tried democratic government, but it doesn't seem able to keep peace and keep us out of trouble. So let's have an emperor. Maybe he can do better.

All these feelings and ideas put together made it possible for a great many people to welcome the Archduke Maximilian and his beautiful, stately wife.

Maximilian, as we learned, had been brought up to

believe that he must govern somewhere, like everybody else in his family. An "Assembly of Notables" had been hastily got together to offer him the throne of Mexico, and he did not see through the fact that this was a little group of conservatives who would have invited *anybody* to Mexico, if it meant getting rid of the hated little Indian Juárez.

We must not forget, either, that much of the scorn and hatred of Juárez was precisely because he had been born in humble circumstances but had not been content to stay so, and because he was dark-skinned, of another race, and from a culture that the rich white Mexicans had dominated for so long that they began to think of them as a permanently enslaved people.

In any case, Maximilian had been summoned. He ordered his elaborate uniforms to be packed, his wife did the same with her regal gowns of fine silk and satin, her necklaces and tiaras, and they embarked for Veracruz. It is interesting to note that, during the voyage, Maximilian, who was to govern a country full of clashing parties, unsettled ideas, poverty-stricken Indian villages that were remnants of once great civilizations, and thousands of subjects who could not even speak Spanish, much less read or write, concerned himself with preparing a booklet of rules of court etiquette.

He did take time, also, to write the president, Benito Juárez, the man he was arriving to depose by force of

French arms, inviting him to cooperate with himself, the archduke.

Juárez received the letter in Monterrey. He answered it because, in his view of orderly, lawful life, letters were courteously answered. However, he was extremely busy, he said, and therefore could not answer the letter meticulously. His activities, he pointed out to the archduke, with some irony, were those of trying to hold his country together under law, through an office to which he had been legally and democratically elected. He said, in his letter: "You tell me that abandoning the succession to a throne in Europe, forsaking your family, your friends, your fortune, and what is most dear to a man, your country, you have come with your wife, Doña Carlota, to distant and unknown lands to satisfy the summons spontaneously made by a people that rest their felicity and their future in you. I am amazed, on the one hand by your generosity, and on the other, my surprise has been great to read in your letter the words, *spontaneous summons,* for I had already perceived that when the traitors of my country appeared at Miramar as a self-constituted commission to offer you the crown of Mexico, with several letters from nine or ten towns of the nation, you saw in all this merely a ridiculous farce, unworthy of serious consideration by an honorable and self-respecting man. [Maximilian at first had not believed that he was wanted in Mexico.] How can I not wonder then, when I see you come to Mexico without any change having been made in the conditions you imposed; how can I not wonder when I see you accept the offers of the traitors, and decorate and employ men like Marquez and Herrán, and surround yourself with all that condemned part of Mexican society?"

(Marquez was the man who had ordered the slaughter of all the sick and the doctors and nurses in the hospital of Tacubaya.)

Juárez went on to say in his letter that he noted that Maximilian offered to escort Juárez safely to Mexico City, with French troops, to confer with him, and offered him some important post in the government that Maximilian proposed to set up.

Juárez's answer was full of bitter scorn and cold courtesy. He wrote: "It is true that contemporary history records the names of great traitors who have broken their oaths, and their promises, and failed their own party, their antecedents, and all that is most sacred to a man of honor, and that in these betrayals the traitor has been guided by an obscure ambition to rule and a base desire to satisfy his own passions and even his own vices; but the present incumbent of the presidency of the Republic of Mexico, who has sprung from the obscure masses of the people, will succumb . . . if in the design of Providence it is ordained that he succumb . . . fulfilling his oath, warranting the hopes of the na-

tion over which he presides, and satisfying the prompt-
ing of his own conscience."

He said, in conclusion: "It is given to men, sir, to
attack the rights of others, to take their property, to
attempt the lives of those who defend their liberty, and
to make of their virtues a crime and of their own vice
a virtue; but there is one thing which is beyond the reach
of perversity, and that is the tremendous verdict of
history. History will judge us."

Of course, Juárez was right, for history has judged.
The kindest historians believe that Maximilian was de-
ceived and that he was well-meaning. To others, it
appears, in the light of years that have gone by, that
he was monumentally stupid to have supposed that the
country as a whole wanted him, and that he could trust
Napoleon III to protect him and his wife. He was wrong
in both instances.

Long before the French emperor finally got tired of
the expense and trouble of maintaining a foreign court
in Mexico—which seemed unable even to finance itself,
let alone get back the French loan and bonds—Maximilian should have realized that even the forces that had
wanted him to come were becoming restive.

The Church, for instance, wanted Maximilian to re-
store Church property at once in the sections of Mexico
already taken by the French, as they made way to conduct Maximilian to Mexico City. The archduke did not

undertake to do this, and the Church became angry with him, for the clergy had lent their support to the idea of a foreign monarchy on the assumption that they would get back the enormous properties they had formerly owned and which the Reform Laws had allowed to revert to the state.

The archduke now held court in a throne room, and was titled emperor; his wife, Carlota, was empress, with a pleased bevy of women surrounding her as her "ladies in waiting." French armies under Marshal Achille Bazaine tried hard to defeat the armies of liberals who were fighting for the cause of the republic, and they often succeeded. The troops of the republic were constantly being defeated and made to retreat and retreat.

Yet Mexico is a very big country, and there was always another Mexican city, not yet taken by the French, where Juárez could preside over a desk or table and execute his duties. He went everywhere with his troops, following in his black coach. In contrast to the glamor of the court in Mexico City, his little entourage was shabby and dusty from traveling. Sometimes they slept in poor ranchos, on straw mats. Often they had only beans to eat, the simple meal of country people who shared what they had.

But as Juárez constantly reminded them, while they had him, the president of Mexico, symbol of the integrity of the state, they were not defeated. Often, he was the only one in his group who was not discouraged, but as he retreated into the northern provinces he worried about the safety of his family. He arranged to send Margarita and the children to the United States, to Washington, D.C., where his friend and representative, Matías Romero, would watch over them.

In sending his family to the United States, Juárez was also depending on his wife to help him. That brave and loyal lady, who had run a little store to keep her family fed while Juárez was in exile, who had walked over the mountains with her children to join him when he got back to Veracruz, was his strongest supporter and stanchest ally.

As it might have been . . .

The throne room in Chapultepec Palace, in Mexico City, is large. Chairs are ranged along the sides of the room, and the pair of "thrones"—elaborate chairs, gilded —dominate one end of the room. There is a large, brilliant chandelier, and though there is no other furniture, the crowd of beautifully dressed women, in hoop-skirted, handsome gowns and flashing jewels, and the men in uniform, or wearing decorations, give the scene an effect of luxury and glamor.

There is a flourish of trumpets, and Maximilian and Carlota enter. He is tall, with blue eyes and a golden beard parted in the middle; he wears a uniform and many decorations. Carlota, the empress, wears oyster-white, draped and gathered with crimson velvet. She wears a necklace, earrings, and a tiara studded with rubies.

They walk slowly through the room, bowing and smiling, and take their places on the thrones. After a time, the emperor rises and takes a paper handed to him by one of his secretaries. There is an immediate silence, after the soft, continuous murmur.

The emperor reads, in a somewhat high voice, in careful, studied Spanish with a strong German accent.

"We have offered Citizen Benito Juárez our most

gracious pardon, and even cooperation, in a spirit of fraternal affection. We have implored that he come to us, surrendering his followers, and consult with us for the good of our beloved Mexico, and we have promised him a position of importance among our advisers and collaborators."

He pauses, so that the public may appreciate his magnanimity.

"He has consistently and stubbornly refused." Now there is a rising murmur of indignation.

"We therefore feel ourselves obliged to give our generals orders to prosecute the war against him and his followers, without mercy, until victory is established."

A shout of approval.

He holds up his hand for silence. "But even when they are defeated, we will not be rancorous, but will deal with our Mexican people, Citizen Benito Juárez among them, with justice and mercy."

The emperor sits down, and then gestures toward the balcony, where musicians are waiting. A Viennese waltz sounds, and as the emperor nods permission, the courtiers begin to dance, whirling about the large throne room to the gentle strains.

THIRTEEN

Margarita

MARGARITA MAZA DE JUÁREZ had been brought up
in a prosperous home and had been taught to do all the
home arts, as every young lady of good family was, in
the provincial capital of Oaxaca. She learned to em-
broider, to make all kinds of delicate sweet desserts,
such as almond cheese, cakes made of ground garbanzos
and honey, and thick, rich, coconut candy. She was
taught elegant, elaborate manners, graceful dancing,
and the way to get in and out of a carriage, lifting her
silk skirts so as to show only a momentary glimpse of
an ankle. She learned all the arts of keeping her hair
glossy with much brushing, and polishing with a silk
cloth; she ground up rice in a metate (stone mortar)
to make a delicate face powder, and she mixed glycerine
and rose water to use as a lotion to keep her hands
smooth.

Her father was a man who had very few of the prejudices of the Mexicans of his day. He took a real interest in the Indian boy who had run away from his mountain home and taken refuge with his sister, Señor Maza's cook. He kept in touch with him as Juárez swept sidewalks, mopped, and did errands for his patron, as he struggled in school and made desperate efforts to learn good Spanish. Señor Maza brought young Señor Juárez to his home, as a welcome visitor and friend when he attained his law degree, and was proud of him and of what he had made of himself.

Margarita was born when Juárez was twenty years old, already a regular visitor at the home. He saw her grow up, and his love for the child became love of the young girl. When she was seventeen, they were married in the cathedral of Oaxaca and began their life together.

Pictures of Margarita reveal a lovely young woman, thoughtful and perhaps dreamy, serious and good. She had reservoirs of strength upon which to draw, for like so many young mothers of her time, she early learned the sorrow of losing children. (She had twelve, in all.)

Her husband, whom she loved devotedly, and greatly admired for his character and his intelligence, was pursued by political enemies before they had been married many years. While he was in exile in New Orleans, Margarita had the whole burden of keeping their home together and raising their children.

She moved to the little town of Etla about ten miles
outside of Oaxaca, set up a small general store, and
worked in it long hours. This was the lady who had been
the governor's wife, used to presiding over state func-
tions, though Juárez had discouraged too much cere-
mony. All the same, the young woman, selling thread
and paper and pots and pans, pencils and soap, running
out once in a while to see a sick child, or coax a fussy
one to eat, must have thought back over the ease and
comfort of those days as the wife of a governor. But she
never complained, at least never in letters to her husband.

She must have kept in close touch with all the very
simple souls of his mountain family and their relatives
and friends, for, when at last Juárez made his way back
to Veracruz, she was guided and protected by them, as
she fled Etla, with her children, and took refuge in the
mountains. Her own life and that of her children had
been threatened, and all she could think of was to get
back to the safety and protection of her husband as fast
as she could. That is why she undertook the journey
with her tiny children, by foot, over the mountain
passes, which are steep and frightening, and sometimes
wreathed in mist, guided by her Indian friends. The
children followed after, whimpering and tired and
frightened; perhaps the smallest one carried in the arms
of some Zapotec relative.

This devoted woman was not animated by a love of law, like her husband. It is obvious that her whole life was lived for love, for love of her husband, loyalty to everything he believed in, and complete devotion to her children.

When Juárez was poor and in trouble, she worked to help him. When he rose to be governor of Oaxaca, or president of the Supreme Court, or president of the republic, there she was, dignified, quiet, perfectly at home in the midst of foreign diplomats and intellectuals.

Juárez, too, was passionately fond of his family, and the tender letters exchanged between him and Margarita give us a touching picture of their private joys and sorrows, while the great events of history whirled around them.

In the United States, under the care of Matías Romero, Margarita and her children lived simply, often on short rations. While the Empress Carlota, in Mexico City, lived surrounded by a large staff—twenty-eight housemaids, five cooks, fifteen errand boys, a stableman, various bakers and pastry cooks, personal maids, hairdressers, and dressmakers—Margarita Juárez looked after her nine children and did all her own work.

She suffered terribly at the death of her little sons José (Pepe) and Antonio. She wrote her husband: "My sorrow at the loss of my sons is so consuming that nothing comforts me. Only time may lessen my suffering.

I am in misery and without much hope of changing this. The hope of seeing you again would be such a great joy, though I am tormented by the fact that when we see each other again, it will be without my two little boys; this idea is killing me and I can't be quiet or tranquil for an instant. The only thing I used to have to help me through trouble was being able to sleep. But now I can't . . . even until five in the morning, I lie awake thinking only of what I have lost. I don't want to grieve you, but it consoles me so much to talk about my sufferings with you because anybody else would be bored and irritated with me, but you would never be that, because you are always considerate. Goodbye, Nito, you know how much I love you. Your wife, Margarita."

This tender mother, sorrowing for the two little boys who died in their childhood, caring for her older daughters, doing the cooking and cleaning, saving her one good dress (bought for her in Monterrey by her husband years before) for occasional ceremonial calls . . . was the person Juárez chose to go and lay the case of the embattled Mexican republic before the American President, Abraham Lincoln.

Accompanied by Matías Romero, shepherded into the Congress by William Seward, Lincoln's Secretary of State, Margarita, in her "best" dress, addressed the Congress of the United States. She was not frightened, because she was doing what her husband needed her to do, and so she did it clearly and calmly. She outlined the series of events which had led to a foreign monarchy in the country, and she asked the American people, through their Congress—the American people committed to freedom and democracy—to recognize that her husband's government was the true and legitimate one in Mexico. She did her part so well that, when she finished, she was given a standing ovation.

Later, General Ulysses S. Grant gave a ball in her honor in Washington, and the lonely wife of the Mexican president, who was still fleeing from French forces and gallantly setting up his government wherever his dusty carriage stood overnight, was accorded every sort of expression of admiration and attention.

The newspapers wrote glowing accounts of her and, perhaps in an attempt to please her, spoke of her elegant appearance. This distressed Margarita very much, for she would not have her struggling husband think she had spent their small store of money, or gone into debt, for dress. She wrote Juárez: "Night before last Romero took me to a reception given by the President, and the papers said I went elegantly dressed and with many diamonds. This is not true; all my elegance consisted of was the dress you bought me in Monterrey. As for the diamonds, I wore only the earrings you gave me one time on my saint's day. I tell you this, because there you are in El Paso, with so much trouble and deprivation, and you must not think I am indulging in luxuries."

Her duty done, Margarita's letters to her husband express her longing to rejoin him. As the news finally became better, and the forces of Juárez began to push the French back steadily and surely, her impatience to be united with him again became almost unbearable.

As it might have been . . .

The Congress of the United States is in full session. All the seats in the great hall are filled with the men who represent the American people, from every section of the vast country. They are quiet, dignified men, in formal attire, many of them bearded, all in middle age or past. There is a raised platform and a table from which a chairman conducts the affairs of the august body. The American flag hangs in drooping, heavy, silk folds, to one side.

There is a buzz of talk and some agitated moving about as the congressmen converse, form small groups, break up, and at last take their seats.

William Seward, the American Secretary of State, a tall, distinguished, gray-haired man, enters the room with a small, plump lady dressed in black silk on his arm. Mr. Seward goes to the speaker's desk and requests silence.

"Gentlemen," he says in ringing tones, "a representative of the republic to the south, of Mexico, has requested a few moments of your time. May I present to you, Doña Margarita Maza de Juárez."

Margarita goes forward, thanks him with a smile and a small bow, and turns her face to the powerful body of

men who have it in their power to recognize or spurn
Benito Juárez's leadership.

She lifts a sweet, clear, rather high voice, and says,
"Gentlemen, I am only a Mexican woman, a simple
wife. But I am the wife of the legally elected president
of Mexico, and in that honorable state, I have come to
tell you of my husband's struggle for freedom because
he cannot come himself."

Imagine a continuation of the speech of the proud
and determined Mexican lady; imagine the attention of
the enormously distinguished and powerful Congress of
the United States.

She finishes her speech. She spreads her small hands
in a gesture of modesty and pleading.

Suddenly a man gets to his feet. Then another. Then
another. In a few moments the Congress is on its feet,
in homage to a Mexican wife; it is applauding, in admiration and in encouragement.

Margarita's eyes stream with tears, but she holds her
head high and murmurs brokenly, again and again,
"Gracias . . . gracias, señores . . . gracias . . .
gracias . . ."

FOURTEEN

The Republic Victorious

J UÁREZ, too, had suffered to hear of the death of his sons. He was worried about his wife's health, which had begun to break under her grief and trouble. And he was constantly fleeing from the forces that pressed upward from the capital, well supplied with food and ammunition by the French francs sent by Napoleon III.

His running just ahead of the armies of Maximilian was not merely a kind of desperate race away from danger. It was part of a real plan, his plan, which he later explained in detail, in a letter he wrote to a young man in France, when the Franco-Prussian war had begun.

He said, in part: "If I were directing the destinies of France, I would proceed no differently from the way I acted in my own beloved country from 1862 to 1867, so that I could triumph, as I did then.

"No enormous bodies of troops, which can move only slowly, and which are difficult to feed because of devastated countryside, and which easily become discouraged with one bad defeat; but armies of fifteen, twenty, or thirty thousand men at the most, tied together in flying columns so that they can quickly go to help each other; engaging the enemy at all hours of the day and night, not waiting for him to set the plan and hour of battle; destroying convoys; giving the enemy no rest, no sleep, no provisions, no arms; leaving occupied country ruined for the invader, so that he can find no food or provision there; and finally obliging him to capitulate, or to retreat, in order to save what is left of his men.

"This is, as you know, the story of the liberation of Mexico. And if the hateful Bazaine, servant of his despised master, the emperor, cares to use some of his spare time at present, the time his treason has procured for him . . . he is the one who can best show your compatriots how guerrilla war is invincible, especially if the guerrilleros fight for the independence of their country."

In the above letter, sent after the troops of the republic had triumphed and Juárez was firmly established as president of Mexico, one can see why Juárez was never discouraged, as his troops retreated and retreated, always going north, before the French forces. It was his firm plan to draw the enemy into territory that could not provision them, to wear them out, to stretch their lines thinner and thinner, and finally to defeat them from sheer misery and discouragement.

Juárez wrote to his representative in Washington to get what aid he could from the American government—loans and arms—but not to compromise one inch of Mexican soil.

Juárez admired President Lincoln, and realized that he had his troubles, with the Civil War raging. He wrote also to Romero, when no money or arms could come his way (except through some private source at the border): "It is enough for us that the North destroy slavery, and *does not recognize Maximilian.*" For, of course, representatives of the Mexican emperor were in Washington, too, hoping to gain recognition from the United States.

Without loans or arms to speak of, Juárez wrote: "We have no choice but to continue the struggle with what we have, as best we can, and as long as we can. This is our duty; time and constancy will help us. Forward, and no fear!"

Besides his own natural patience and stubbornness, Juárez clung to his ideal of the law. And the law, for him, meant the will of the people, as expressed in a constitution, which they could change at their will . . . not the rules laid down by any autocratic or self-styled ruler. He believed in the consent of the governed, which

is the strongest democratic principle to come out of our
modern thought about government, and which takes
precedence over many other attitudes which possibly
could settle problems faster, or do more immediate good
in certain circumstances. But without the consent of the
governed and their participation in the selection of
authority, all else is dictatorship of one sort or another
. . . of one man, or a few, or a party.

Juárez waited with his immovable Indian patience for
Lincoln to finish up his war and solve his problems.
Then, he knew, Lincoln would help him. But Lincoln
was assassinated not long after the signing of the peace
at Appomattox. Juárez felt this blow keenly. Reverses of
his armies in the north occurred, and he, as representative of the republic, was advised to take refuge across
the border in El Paso, because if he was captured, the
enemy would surely triumph. He went across reluctantly, and at the first opportunity returned, for it
worried and saddened him to be a government in exile.

Even some of the men who had supported Juárez,
and fought for him and with him, began to desert. He
was undismayed. "It does our cause no good to have
discouraged men in it," he said. He stood firm, as always,
resting all his confidence in the law and the rights it
had conferred upon him as president. General Ortega,
who had been named president of the Supreme Court
and was therefore, according to law, the man who would

succeed to the presidency should Juárez die or be unable to finish out his office, betrayed him.

Ortega, after trying in vain to get Juárez to agree to compromising with the French empire, had gone to the United States, actually deserting, although he claimed that he had gone to seek more army supplies. Juárez had pretended to believe this, but in his heart, he knew that Ortega had abandoned him. Juárez remembered Ortega's efforts to convince him to give in and to accept a high post from Maximilian. But Juárez answered, "Let the enemy conquer and rob us, if such be our destiny; but we must never *legalize a crime* by delivering voluntarily what is demanded of us by force."

The words made clear for all time what Juárez thought of any sort of compromise.

Then, while the republicans were still fighting—with their backs to the wall, almost, for they had been forced to the very border of the United States—a legal problem of great importance came up. Juárez's *legal* term as president came to an end. And Ortega, who should then have succeeded him, had fled.

Juárez solved this problem by proclaiming, by presidential decree, an extension of his tenure as president, until such time as free elections could be held in the country (obviously, not while Maximilian was on the throne and the country so divided). Considering at last that Ortega had really failed his country, Juárez had him indicted as a military deserter. This meant that, when and if Ortega returned to Mexico, he would have to stand trial and explain why, against his president's orders, he had left the country, deserted his post, and gone to live in the United States.

While Juárez still clung to his ideals of law and tried to solve his problems in a calm, unprejudiced, and judicial way, two things happened that helped him.

The first was a decree signed by Maximilian, which proclaimed that any Mexican citizen caught bearing arms, was to be shot within twenty-four hours without a trial and without appeal. Also, any person or group which harbored a Mexican bearing arms was to be fined and imprisoned.

Now this decree merely put into words what had actually been the case during the progress of the war, but it helped Juárez's cause because it incensed Mexican citizens. In such troublesome times, many Mexican citizens, not embroiled in the fighting, trying to work to keep their families together, carried arms. Besides, this order from a foreigner suddenly struck them all as arrogant and not to be borne. A great tide of sympathy for the republican armies in the north swept through the country.

There are apologists for Maximilian who insist that he was persuaded by bad councilors to sign the odious October decree; the fact is, he signed it, and thus put an end to anyone's thinking he wanted to collaborate with Juárez, as he had said in several letters to the Mexican president.

The other change that helped Juárez and the tired, ragged soldiers who fought for the republic was the withdrawal of the support of Napoleon III because he had become tired of the whole Mexican "adventure." Now it became clear that even Maximilian knew that the Mexican people as a whole did not want him, because he wrote to Napoleon demanding that he still be given the support of the French troops. And he threatened to sell the Isthmus of Tehuantepec to the Americans, in order to get money enough to keep himself in power, if Napoleon did indeed withdraw his army. But the threats, meant to frighten Napoleon (who did not want the United States to get a part of Mexico, where they might build a canal), had no effect, and Napoleon did call back his armies.

When this happened, the republicans took heart and gained several victories in the north. Maximilian's troops were pushed back. Far away in New York, Margarita Juárez, longing to return to Mexico and her husband, made plans to join him. She was not sure how to come, because she wanted very much to bring back with her, in their coffins, the bodies of her two sons.

The Empress Carlota went to France to beg Napoleon to continue to help with men and money; she saw him three times, and did her best, but he had made up his mind to wash his hands of Mexico. He was also worried and frightened because of the growing power of Prussia under Bismarck. He felt that the French would have to fight Germany before long, and he was right.

Maximilian, in the meantime, stopped trying to govern; he amused himself in the pretty little town of Cuernavaca, where he had a mistress, known as "la India bonita" (the pretty Indian) and a son by her. He then took most of his treasures with him and made his way over to Orizaba, not far from Veracruz, where a frigate awaited him, ready to carry him away to safety.

Yet, for some reason, he vacillated. Both his mother and Carlota were unable to accept the idea that their dear Max would not be an emperor any more, only an archduke again. They were full of the European mystique about royalty and the necessity of holding titles and thrones. Maximilian couldn't make up his mind.

Eventually, he decided to make one last effort. He went into the field as a commander of troops. This last move, of course, signed his death warrant, for under military law he thus became a real usurper, not merely a tool of the French armies. When he was captured at last, he was therefore tried as a traitor.

Juárez was with the liberal troops of the republic who were fighting their way south. In Zacatecas, his men captured an order from Maximilian to his general

Miramón, ordering him to court-martial Juárez and his
ministers if he caught them, but to refer the sentence to
Maximilian. One does not know whether, should such
a capture have been made, Maximilian would have pardoned and exiled Juárez or have had him shot. Anyway,
he intended to have a hand in whatever was done to
Juárez; he wanted to have a look at him. No doubt he
was curious to see his implacable though steadily courte-
ous enemy. He had tried time and again to make some
sort of compromise with Juárez, which the Mexican
president had always resolutely refused.

The French people, who were becoming tired of all
the expense and trouble of keeping Maximilian on the
throne in Mexico, were interested in the personality of
Juárez, and Napoleon asked one of his soldiers who had
been in the Mexican campaigns about it. Lieutenant
Colonel Brissonet wrote to the French emperor: "I see
general opinion taking shape every day, in favor of
Juárez, and I have no doubt that after our departure
[the French army in Mexico, keeping Maximilian on
the throne], he will again be placed at the head of the
government of this country . . . I know and feel that
the French government cannot enter into open relations with Juárez. Since he is the only one who can give
us the guarantees that we must demand, we shall have
to have recourse to him in the end . . . Juárez is not
the man who has been so decried in France; he is a

Mexican and has many of the defects of his race, undoubtedly, but few of his countrymen have so many
qualities. He is disinterested, he is ready to efface himself if the interests of his country so demand, he is anything but bloodthirsty . . ."

Juárez, on his sixtieth birthday, wrote to his wife in
New York, commenting on the departure of Napoleon
III's troops and the general success of the republic:
"Mexico will be free of the triple yoke of a state religion,
privileged classes, and oppressive treaties with Euro-
pean powers."

The war went on. When Juárez and the liberal army
came into Zacatecas, which had been abandoned by
French troops, the people gave Juárez a cane, which
had been bought with money donated in gratitude to
their president. But the French came back, and Juárez,
with his men, had to hurry out of the city and go north
again. However, in time, the liberals retook the city;
the first thing Juárez did was ask for his cane back.

Then Miramón, Maximilian's general, was defeated
in battle, and Maximilian was bottled up in the city of
Querétaro. The liberal army put it under a siege which
lasted one hundred days. In the meantime, Marquez,
the assassin of Tacubaya, burst out of the city and went
to Mexico City to try to get help. None was forthcoming.

Juárez, though he was steadily making his way south
toward the capital city with his victorious fighters, had

troubles enough all along the way. Santa Anna, who had brought Mexico to disaster more than once, with typical flamboyance offered his sword to Juárez. Juárez gently but firmly declined, and advised him, for the good of his country, to stay far away.

Then Ortega reappeared. This man, legally the president (because Juárez's term had finished), had deserted his country and gone into hiding in the United States. Now, with victory obvious as the French army had left the country and Maximilian's generals were being defeated, he demanded to be installed as president. He returned to the country, but Juárez ordered him jailed as a deserter—which, of course, he was.

However, Juárez's strong legal conscience caused him to announce that as soon as he returned to the capital, he would order free elections, and this he did.

As it might have been . . .

The plain outside the city of Zacatecas, which lies in a cleft, with cliffs and hills on either side. After having held the city, and then lost it, the victorious liberal troops have captured it again, and the conservative French armies which support Maximilian have retreated pell-mell toward the south.

Tired soldiers in motley uniforms—some without coats, some without caps, others wearing the straw sombreros of the north, all tired and weary—are slogging along the road. Inside the city there is blessed silence after all the shooting, though groans of the wounded can be heard. As a black carriage enters the city, in the midst of the last liberal soldiers, all the church bells of the city begin a jubilant clanging, and to this glorious sound of victory, Mexico's president proceeds, in the carriage behind tired horses, into the main square. He turns to speak to his people . . . a sturdy figure, hatless; his hair is lank and a bit too long; he needs a barber.

"Citizens," he says in a ringing voice that everyone can hear, "I have come back for my cane!"

A great cry of glee breaks out, there are "Vivas," and a little girl, about five years old, her hair in two black braids tied with pink ribbons, emerges from the crowd.

She is a bit shy, but someone pushes her from behind, and a fine cane, with a silver knob, is given to her. She starts up the stairs toward the president of Mexico. She holds out the cane. Smiling, bowing to her, he takes it, and then he leans down to kiss the child's cheek.

"Citizens! I have my cane, and the French are defeated! Go home to supper and your beds! Long live Mexico!"

The jubilant cry is echoed by the crowd, and shouted again and again, as Juárez turns, and slowly, wearily, climbs the last steps. He disappears inside the Palace of the Governor, in Zacatecas.

FIFTEEN

The Final Struggles

M EANWHILE, besieged Querétaro fell. Maximilian was made captive, with his two generals Tomás Mejía and Miramón. These two military men were held for trial in a military court, which was strictly according to the rules of warfare; Juárez knew the rules.

Maximilian wrote a letter to Juárez in San Luis Potosí, asking for a personal interview, but Juárez, who had been on the run with his liberal army and who would have been tried at once by court-martial if he had been captured by Maximilian's men, did not feel it necessary to grant this request. However, he did everything a fair judge should do. He provided Maximilian with lawyers to defend him. One of those lawyers was a man who had always opposed the empire; nevertheless, he did his best in defense of the captured emperor.

A case was made that Maximilian should be looked

on merely as a factional or political opponent of Juárez, because he had stayed on, even after the French army was gone, and because he had proclaimed himself "a Mexican" and wore Mexican dress sometimes. But Maximilian was tried and condemned to die.

Now Juárez was subjected to every sort of scene and sentimental assault from people who still loved the idea of royalty, and who, despite all the bloodshed, looked on Maximilian as merely misguided, not as a foreigner who had tried to seize power by force of arms.

One lady, the Princess Salm-Salm, pleaded with Juárez on her knees, but he courteously raised her and told her that he could not do anything to save Maximilian; this was a matter for the Mexican people to decide. Maximilian had been condemned to death by a proper court, according to law, and had had adequate defense. Juárez told the princess that it was not he who would take Maximilian's life, but the law and the people. If the sentence were not carried out, the people would still demand Maximilian's life, and Juárez's as well. Nevertheless, she reported that Juárez's eyes filled with tears before she left, and his aide, who was present, said that Juárez suffered very much at having to sign the execution orders for two Mexican citizens, Miramón and Mejía.

The whole world agitated about the case, which was discussed in European and American newspapers everywhere. Many great men, among them Victor Hugo and Garibaldi, both of whom had sympathized with Juárez's ordeal in the long struggle against the imposed empire, begged him to be an example to the world, to abolish the death penalty, and to let Maximilian go free. Juárez stood by what he believed in—the processes of law. If in due course the people of Mexico abolished the death penalty, he would respect it. But they had not done so, and all his instincts were against any one-man government . . . even his own.

He was stung into answering, though, when William Seward, who had defended his cause before the American Congress, wrote a condescending message in which he told Juárez that "carrying out the death sentence on Maximilian will not raise Mexico in the esteem of civilized nations." Juárez wrote back: "The Mexican government, which has given numerous proofs of its humanitarian principles and its sentiments of generosity, is also obliged to remember its duty to the Mexican people."

He wrote to Victor Hugo: "Impatient patriots want everything to be settled at once, but this is impossible. The government continues to proceed slowly with the firm determination to do what best benefits the country, and without being influenced by personal vengeance, misguided pity, or any foreign threats. We have fought for the independence and autonomy of Mexico, and it must be a reality."

Though far-off writers asked for compassion, and kings and princes begged for it, offering their word of honor that no other prince would come to Mexico's shores to try to start an empire, what reason had the battered troops of Juárez to believe any of them? The thing had happened; it might happen again. "Put not thy trust in princes" was part of the army's strong belief, and Juárez was surrounded by the army that had fought and bled and died to try to drive out the usurper. They were not likely to feel pity for Maximilian the moment he was captured.

Porfirio Díaz, a young general who had done much for the liberal cause by defending the south and by keeping the armies of Maximilian away from the escape route via Veracruz, wrote to Juárez that, if Maximilian were not executed, according to the sentence of the court which had tried him, "he [Díaz] would not be responsible for what the army might do in the capital."

Maximilian, though he had been a poor governor, took his place before the firing squad with great dignity, and behaved without bitterness or contempt. He had wanted to rule like a prince; in the end, he died like one.

In Europe, there are places where Juárez is still not forgiven for not having pardoned Maximilian. In

Vienna, there is a funeral plaque commemorating Maximilian, and under it are the words "Assassinated in
Mexico." The Mexican government has tried for many
years to persuade the family owning the plaque to
change "assassinated" to "executed," but so far without
results.

Perhaps the most modern comment on the execution
of Maximilian was made by Georges Clemenceau, the
famous "Tiger" of France, who was later to stand up
against German invasion in 1914. "They are always
charming, these people" (meaning the aristocrats), he
wrote. "They smile . . . how delightful! They weep
. . . how pathetic! . . . They let you live . . . what
exquisite kindness! They crush you! Blame their un-
fortunate position. I have no pity for those people. To
pity the wolf is to commit a crime against the lamb!"

Maximilian died with his generals on June 19, 1867.
On June 21, Mexico City surrendered, and on July 13,
Juárez came back into the city, completely re-estab-
lished as the president of a free republic.

He made a speech, urged moderation and hard work
on everyone, and said the words which are always
quoted, again and again, as his formula for peace:
"Among nations, as among individuals, respect for the
rights of others is peace."

A final comment on the whole struggle was written
by the Spaniard Emilio Castelar. He said: "There was

nothing worthy or honorable in the expedition to Mexico, neither in its preparation nor in its end nor in any
of the persons who took part in it; what was very great
and very honorable was the opposition that fought and
overcame it . . . the faith and strength of the Mexican
people, and the imposing dignity and the iron will of
Juárez."

As it might have been . . .

In an unadorned room in the Palace of the Governor of Querétaro, Benito Juárez sits at a desk, studying the papers which have just been handed him by a uniformed orderly.

Juárez looks up at the orderly, a boy not more than seventeen.

"The military court has condemned Maximilian, Miramón, and Mejía to death by firing squad," he tells the young man.

The boy's face moves in a grimace of pain, or compassion.

Juárez sits, impassive, solemn.

"Señor Presidente!"

Juárez looks up.

The guard at the door of his room bows and says, "There are women here, pleading for the life of Maximilian. They beg to speak to you."

Juárez considers. "I will receive the citizens who have some business with me tomorrow. I cannot be disturbed now."

Quietly he reads through the papers ordering the death sentences. For a long time he sits, immobile, thinking, considering, making no move to sign the papers.

Then he speaks to the orderly, in a conversational tone. "I must sign these. They are the orders of the court. These men were fairly tried, and sentence has been passed. I could weep, indeed I do . . ." and his eyes glitter with tears for a moment . . . "for the Mexicans who must stand up and die with the archduke. For Miramón and Mejía, who leave families, who were citizens who chose a wrong path.

"I can weep for Maximilian, also, for his stubborn foolishness and vanity.

"But I weep more, and will weep in the future, for all the men who fought and bled and died, so that Mexico could remain a republic, governed by law and by her own people.

"For those who fell, and all their sorrowing families, I will weep until the day I die."

And he takes up the pen and signs the sentences.

SIXTEEN

Last Years

ONE MONTH after entering Mexico City in triumph, Juárez called for free elections. Not only did he plan a number of reforms as to how elections were to be carried out, he also recommended giving the vote to the clergy. But the liberal party in the congress would have none of these reforms, which were then voted down.

In the elections, Juárez was the winner and became president for a second term. This was to be expected, though Lerdo de Tejada and Porfirio Díaz ran against him. The country was divided into many conflicting groups, even among the liberals, now that there was no longer a common enemy to unite them.

Juárez, however, went straight ahead and carried out the instructions of his legal and just conscience.

He voluntarily gave back all the dictatorial powers that had been given him during the war.

He gracefully accepted defeat when the vote went against him on his proposed reforms.

He humbly accepted his constitutional restrictions and never referred to any of the military triumphs which had been carried out under his instructions.

But this peaceful and humble person, unglamorous in his black suit, was not an exciting leader, and people like excitement. He then did something that made many people annoyed: he asked for and collected his wages, as president, for the years when he had not been paid.

The sum, actually, was a pittance, considered against what the country was in a position to pay, but again . . . this act seemed entirely too vulgar and commonplace for many of the people who had still not forgotten the glitter and aristocratic grace of an emperor's court. Nobody stopped to think that Juárez had a family of seven children to take care of and educate, and that he was scrupulously honest in money matters and not likely to gather in money for a personal fortune from outside sources, as so many politicians did. Also, Juárez's wife was ill, and growing steadily worse.

Poor Margarita had borne twelve children and had lost two young sons as well as three infants. Her health broke, and she could no longer hold off the inroads of the disease which was to take her life when she was only forty-five. She died of cancer, January 2, 1871.

It is said that Juárez was inconsolable when Mar-

garita died. He would allow no one to touch her body
but himself. He laid her in her coffin, and gave her one
last kiss. He did not long survive her, but his final
months were full of work and duty.

He had many problems to trouble him. The main one
—and it continues to be a problem as the Mexican popu-
lation constantly grows—was the plight of the country
people, the agricultural workers, the peons. Most of
these were semiattached to great land holdings—semiattached because they were dependent on the patron
for their livelihood, their pitiful wages. Juárez, dedicated to law as he was, could find no way to help them.
The revolutionary idea of "expropriation" of privately
held lands, to give out anew to the poor peons, was to
come much later, in an attempt to solve part of the land
problem.

There were many other reasons for the general misery
in the countryside. For one thing—and this was what
prompted Porfirio Díaz, later, to give out concessions to
foreign engineering companies—the country lacked
means of communication. It needed highways; it needed
railroads. And the intellectuals of the country, who had
supported the long struggle to expel the French, began
to perceive a greater danger in the strong power to the
north, the United States, which still seemed to look upon
Mexico as a country that should be "taken over" by
Americans and "developed."

Growing unpopularity marked Juárez's last years. After finishing his term as president in 1871, he announced he would run again. History shows that this was a mistake on his part, one of several errors of judgment which he made in his final years. These errors gave ammunition to the political opposition, which had begun to look for new leaders, new faces, new blood.

In the first place, Juárez was elected by such a small majority of votes that the election was cast into the congress, where again, he won, but by an extremely small margin. He might have done well to accept this and to step down. But a man who has been indispensable for many years finds it hard to believe that he is no longer so. An insistence on doing things as they have always been done is a sign of age, and Juárez was growing old. Eager young Mexicans wanted him out of the way, so that they could begin to make changes they felt were needed. Or perhaps many of them simply felt that he had been in power long enough. In politics the world over, "Time for a change" is the cry heard very often when one man has held the reins of government for too many years.

The same two men had run against him once more—Lerdo de Tejada and Porfirio Díaz—and Díaz claimed that he had won. He started a revolt, and began a rallying cry of "No Re-election!" (This motto is now part of all Mexican official papers, but the ironies of history are curious. Díaz, who originated this cry, was himself to be re-elected many times, in years to come, before a revolution in 1910 actually established the rule of no re-election.)

Juárez, seeing mutinies developing everywhere, again asked the congress for extraordinary powers, and he put down the riots and rebellions sternly. He even used the hated "leva," or forced military service, to get soldiers to keep the peace, and for this he was loathed by many people.

He had seen the state of misery and poverty the country was in as he had traveled up and down it. Undoubtedly, he felt that peace was what Mexico needed after so many years of fighting and bloodshed, and he was prepared to put down each disturbance as it occurred and see to it that it went no further. This was probably sound thinking, but he had been the champion of liberty for so long that the new attitude did not become him. And whereas before he had been admired and respected, now resentment began to build up against him. His iron will, which had saved the country from a foreign empire, no longer pleased people who wanted changes and was now called insane stubbornness.

Juárez never showed, in any way, that he cared about having lost his popularity. He simply went his way. But he was old, a lonely, grieving widower, and ill. As was typical of his character, he asked for no sympathy and continued working as long as he was able to stand. Many people believed that his unbending severity in his last years and his illness were both caused by the loss of his wife, who had been so dear to him and a true collaborator in all his policies.

After several cardiac attacks, Juárez asked his doctor, "Is my illness mortal?" He was told that it was. Thereafter, he simply continued working until the last attacks, when the doctors could no longer bring him back to consciousness. His steady courage through all these painful attacks amazed all who knew him. But they were typical of him and of the courage of his race.

He died on July 18, 1872.

As it might have been . . .

In a bedroom in the presidential palace in Mexico City, Juárez lies dead upon the bed, covered by a sheet. There is a heavy, sad silence in the room. Footsteps may be heard, the creak of doors opening and closing. Darkness is falling, and the flames of the thick white candles at the head and at the foot of the bed softly illuminate the room.

Two men enter.

"You have done this before?" whispers one. The other, who is carrying a large satchel, answers, also very softly, in respect for the dead man, "Oh yes. Often."

Two men and two weeping women are sitting to one side of the room, keeping watch. One of the men who entered pulls back the sheet from the dead face.

"What is this? What is he doing?" cries one of the women hysterically.

"Hush. He will make the death mask. So that sculptors and everyone can know what Benito Juárez really looked like."

Now the woman has begun to sob convulsively.

"Hush, hush!"

"But it's so sad! To die like that . . . all alone . . . working . . . no one to comfort him . . . No one to mourn him . . ."

The man who has come to make the death mask has got his materials ready and is about to begin his work. He looks up and answers the sobbing woman. "Ah, you're wrong there! Maybe he died alone . . . but he will be mourned! All Mexico will mourn him . . . and someday . . . the whole world!

"Because he was good. He stood firm for the law . . . through everything. The world will remember . . ."

AFTERWORD

As Juárez wrote to Maximilian, History is the final judge of man and of movements. Time and history, indeed, have seen to it that the iron-willed Juárez, the Zapotec, is beloved of all the people in the Americas. He holds the title conferred upon him by all Latin America, "Benemérito de las Americas."

Many people think of Juárez as the Mexican Lincoln, and in a sense he was. He and Lincoln (both civilians), held their countries together and brought them safely through civil war. Both were modest and unassuming, and came from poor families. Both rose to eminence through their own persistent intellectual progress. Both men's lives marked the beginning of new growth for their countries. Both represented, in their own lives, the end of a falsely glamorous aristocratic image. They were democrats in the true sense of the word.

Juárez, moreover, in the years of his presidency, was the symbol of a new, emerging Mexico; after Juárez, it was recognized that Mexico was no longer a colony of Spain, even in traditions and psychology. The country is a new one, because it is populated by a new people, the *Mexicans*, who are neither Spanish nor Indian, but a proud amalgam of both.

Few men have the opportunity to save their country from foreign despoilment, to set up laws guaranteeing equal rights to all men, and to set the course of government on a road to freedom. Juárez was such a man. He saw his duties, and carried them out with steadfast courage.

When he spoke of history judging men's acts, he spoke truth, but he was far too modest to see himself as the great symbol in history which he became.

He was a man who looked to law, and strict observance of law, to settle most of mankind's problems. His faith in law held firm until his death, and it has become, for all young people of the Americas, an ideal to cherish and live by.

PRINCIPAL SOURCES

ALATORRE, ANGELES MENDIETA, *Margarita Maza de Juárez*

CRUZ, EVERARDO MORENO, *Juárez Jurista*

ENRÍQUEZ, ANDRÉS MOLINA, *Historia de México*

FRÍAS Y SOTO, HILARIÓN, *La Intervencion & El Imperio* (a refutation, with documents, of *The True Juárez*, by Francisco Bulnes)

ROEDER, RALPH, *Juárez and His Mexico*

TAMAYO, JORGE, *Epistolario de Benito Juárez*

UGARTE, JOSÉ BRAVO, *Compendio de Historia de México*

Various essays, interviews, and consultations

INDEX